A MEMOIR OF AN AMERICAN DREAM FAMILY

I'M ALMOST
HISTORY

RICHARD STOEBEL

HALLARD
PRESS

Richard Stoebel

Editor: Joyce Wedge
Cover Design by Hallard Press LLC/John W Prince
Page Design, Typography & Production by Hallard Press LLC/John W Prince

Published by Hallard Press LLC.
www.HallardPress.com   Info@HallardPress.com   352-775-1143

Bulk copies of this book can be ordered at Info@HallardPress.com

Printed in the United States of America

Library of Congress Control Number: 2020908116

ISBN: 978-1-951188-08-5

0102030405

DEDICATION

To my wife, Brenda, thank you for always being there with encouragement and understanding. You are my best friend and confidant. I could not have accomplished anything in married life without you.

To my parents in Heaven, who guided me in my formative years, thank you for allowing me to be anything in life that I wanted to be. It was a job well done.

TABLE OF CONTENTS

1. AN INTRODUCTION

Have you ever had experiences in life where you've said: "I could write a book about that." I'll bet you have! That statement started me thinking about some of the things that I have seen and done in my lifetime. Maybe my children and grandchildren might be interested in reading about my story. One day recently I began to write it all down.

My philosophy has always been that life is like a river, just go with the flow. If you buck the system when a proverbial door opens, then you may miss an opportunity, and the door closes. You can influence which direction you take in life to some degree, but a lot of it has been decided for you by a higher power. I really believe that. Some of it is luck.

Perhaps you may have avoided a serious accident by a twist of fate. Perhaps you were destined to meet and marry a certain person. Maybe you had the good fortune to not marry someone who may have been a toxic match for you. I was lucky enough to find my soul mate, Brenda. We married in

1969 and then celebrated our 25th anniversary by renewing our vows. We renewed them again on our 50th anniversary and I tell people that I loved this girl so much that I married her three times!

Brenda and me renewing our vows at our 50th wedding anniversary, April 18, 2019.

A friend of ours told us that he married three times also —but it was to three different women! I guess I'm just a lucky guy. Here we are in a Florida retirement community called The Villages (TV), living the lifestyle that we all dream of, but which our parents never knew. I suppose that there may be some luck involved because we are able to retire comfortably. Brenda was always a very sensible girl who saw the value of saving for a rainy day and, ultimately, retirement. We saved a lot of money by doing almost everything ourselves like housework, yard work, car maintenance, plumbing, and electrical repairs.

We pride ourselves on never having hired a house cleaning person. Heck, if we had, we would have cleaned the house before they arrived! But now, in retirement, we do hire out most of the yard work and major projects to local experts. We still clean the house together though, and still do most of the house repairs. It's hard to let go of our self-reliant past.

Now our life is filled with a variety of activities and our calendar is always full. We love to dance. Actually, Brenda loves to dance but we made a deal. If I took dance lessons with her, she would take golf lessons for me. As it turns out, I developed a liking for dancing also and our favorite style is the east coast swing. Cha-cha, waltz, two step, country line, and country partner dancing are all part of our repertoire as well. We had taken up country dancing years ago and began taking lessons again in TV. I'm still not sure to this day if Brenda has totally embraced golf. If not, she sure puts on a good show.

I like shooting. I have been a shooting enthusiast all my life and just recently got back into it, mostly with handguns. A new Shooters World just opened nearby and it is a first-class facility. I try to go there at least once a week. I have been an NRA certified pistol instructor for more than twenty-five years and still enjoy teaching the discipline of this sport when I get a chance.

I taught our kids how to safely handle and shoot all types of guns. My daughter, Kimberly, is like Annie Oakley with a handgun and my son, Brett, is a police range officer who is now in charge of training other officers in his department. I guess the apple doesn't fall too far from the tree!

Me at The Villages polo field with my radio-controlled Cessna 188 agricultural model. Notice the big smile!

I have been an airplane enthusiast all my life too, so it goes without saying that I still enjoy all things with wings! Lately, my flying has been limited to radio-controlled planes. We have a beautiful facility nearby which is organized by the E-fliers Club here in The Villages. We use one of three local polo fields for flying and the aircraft are limited to electric power only. Of course, you just can't have one airplane so I have four in the hanger (garage). Some of my flying buddies are a little over the top, however, and have twenty or thirty planes.

What's better than having a hot rod? Having two, of course! I am the proud owner of a 1930 Ford roadster which I bought from a guy in California nineteen years ago. My other hot rod is a 1932 Ford 5-window coupe which I built over an eight-year period. Both cars are original steel and, of course, have been modified to go fast.

Having gone to a lot of car shows, both local and national, my interest and fun now is to just drive these cars around the community on a nice day and give rides to the kids, grandkids, and friends. When driving the cars (which one to choose at any given time is a big decision) the waves, smiles, and thumbs-up from admiring folks are very gratifying.

Have you heard of pickleball? It is a game we were introduced to when we first came to The Villages on a lifestyle program visit in 2003. We took up the game seriously in 2010, quickly became addicted and we play almost every day.

The game is played on a modified tennis court using a racquet similar to a large ping-pong (table tennis) paddle and a wiffle ball about the size of a baseball. When we were Snowbirds, spending our summer months in Connecticut, there was no place to play so we became ambassadors for the USA Pickleball Association (USAPA) and introduced the game into several towns in central Connecticut. I suppose it was self-serving because it gave us a place to play when we were up north.

Now the game has spread all over the country and

has gone international as well. I taught pickleball 101 in The Villages for seven years and enjoyed introducing new people to the game. In Connecticut a new player walked up to me one day and said: "You were my pickleball instructor in Florida"! We have been good friends ever since and we have met many hundreds of fine people participating in this sport. My wife's nickname is "THE HAMMER"—boy, can she hit the ball hard!

Brenda and I had gone to a pickleball court one evening to practice. We met another couple, Chris and Pat Beltrami, who were just learning the game. They had big smiles and we liked them right away. After practicing and playing for a while, we decided to go out for dinner. We have been the best of friends ever since.

I have been playing golf off and on ever since I was sixteen years old, but I have never had a hole in one! I told my wife if she gets a hole in one before I do, I will never play with her again. I have had a couple of eagles, but never saw them go in the hole because they were blind shots. The elusive hole in one may never happen in my lifetime. Maybe, just maybe, I'm not that good a golfer? Oh well, I will keep trying. I play championship courses twice a week and executive once a week… usually with my wife and another couple. I am actually scoring better than ever before.

It may be that equipment is better now or perhaps I concentrate more in my old age and having to work for a living is no longer clouding my head. The game can be frustrating at times but that one good shot keeps bringing

me back. I just shot my third eagle recently and, this time, I actually watched it go in the hole! It was almost like a hole in one.

We have a hot tub and salt water pool on our lanai, so I get to swim every day if I so choose. My routine is to jump into the hot tub early in the morning and then into the pool to swim fifty laps. Later in the day I usually do another fifty laps. My wife challenged me one day saying: "Give me ten laps, boy"! I complied and it felt so good that I worked my way up to one hundred laps, which I now do every day. I swim an average of around thirteen miles a month.

Since our pool is private, what the heck do you need a bathing suit for? The word is out that almost everybody who has a pool in our community swims sans bathing suit. For us old, matured body people, the saying is "I DON'T SKINNY DIP, I CHUNKY DUNK." My current favorite house rules sign next to the pool is "MEN… NO SHIRT, NO SERVICE. WOMEN … NO SHIRT, FREE DRINKS."

We thought that it might be a nice idea to have bicycles for a little extra exercise when we are in between activities, so we picked up a couple of twenty-four speed bikes from the local shop. We were told that you must wear a helmet when biking to prevent head injuries which, apparently, are the most common type of injury in this sport. We bought some economy helmets and put them on to pedal around our community on cool mornings or calm evenings.

Before long, we were invited by a neighborhood group to join them in an off-site ride in a neighboring town. We loaded the bikes into our SUV and headed out with the gang. During our ride and nearing the completion of it, one of our more experienced lady bikers skidded on some sand, overcorrected and went down, hitting her head on the pavement. She was knocked out cold and an ambulance was called. She subsequently recovered at the hospital and was home the next day.

Inspection of her helmet revealed it was cracked but it ultimately saved her life, or at a minimum, from a serious injury. Needless to say, the next day we were at the bike shop purchasing the best quality helmets that they offered. Experienced riders tell us that it is not a question of if you will be thrown from your bicycle, it is a matter of when. Wise words!

We have two archery ranges in our community. I used to shoot years ago with my son, Brett, and competed in the very first Connecticut State Games. That was thirty-five years ago. I was proficient enough at the time to win a gold medal in the men's masters division. My equipment had been stored away for most of the ensuing years until just recently when a friend expressed a desire to take the introductory archery 101 course offered for free here in TV. So, we took the course together, not long ago, and found the instruction very enjoyable. I have since tuned up my old equipment and I'm planning to return to the range for some long delayed practice.

Are you starting to see a trend here? All these things to do and so little time left to do them. My dad used to tell me that when you try to do a bunch of things, you will never do any of them well. "Jack of all trades, master of none" he used to say.

He was right but I feel that if I can do all these activities well enough to have fun and be safe, I am a happy camper. At this point in my life I am trying to squeeze it all in. When we were working and raising a family, we just did not have the time. Now we are going for it.

Such is our life in retirement. When we were transitioning to life in Florida we were SNOWFLAKES. Then we became SNOWBIRDS. And finally, we became FROGS!

Snowflakes can be defined as those who come to Florida for the coldest winter months of January, February and March. They might rent a house or villa to spend those cold months in a relatively warm climate.

Snowbirds are next in the progression to come south, not only to escape winter, but to escape income taxes in their home state. If you become a Florida resident and stay a minimum of six months plus one day, you can avoid those taxes.

Then there is the dreaded Frog. This means you have sold your property up north, are now a full-time resident of Florida, and will probably croak here.

I've heard people refer to Florida as "God's waiting room." I prefer to look at it as a melting pot of people from all walks of life who simply want to fully enjoy their retirement years in a nice environment. We have friends here who were military generals, rear admirals, IT specialists, pentagon employees, business owners, engineers, bus drivers, and firemen but we are all equal in retirement. It is the Life of Riley, so to speak. The Villages advertises itself as

Florida's friendliest hometown and we are definitely 'Living the Lifestyle.'

I've been witness to some very interesting things in my lifetime. I've done some crazy things and had some scary moments. I've mostly learned from my mistakes, but my dad used to tell me "learn from the mistakes of others because you will never live long enough to make them all yourself." He should have been a philosopher! I've laughed, loved, cried, and accumulated some great memories. Now that I am almost history, I'd like to share some of them with you.

2. THE EARLY DAYS

I was born in the small industrial town of Clinton, Massachusetts on December 27, 1944. My parents were factory workers and left school somewhere around the eighth grade. They never attended college or, for that matter, high school.

My father, Henry Arthur Stoebel, was born February 10, 1903, the year that the Wright brothers first flew their plane at Kill Devil Hills in North Carolina. I remember my dad telling me that because flying was all the rage when he was really young, he made an attempt to jump off the back porch roof with an umbrella. You can guess the outcome — the umbrella folded and he crashed! Probably the one and only attempt at flying that he tried, I would guess.

My father's parents both immigrated from Germany, he was one of eight children, and the youngest. His father died when he was thirteen years old. I remember my father telling me that his father was struck from behind by a bicycle while coming home from getting a haircut. He hit his head on the pavement and two weeks later died from complications of that injury.

Now fatherless, an older brother, Frank, took my father under his wing and helped him through his formative years. Because the head of the household was no longer able to provide for the family, the kids were expected to chip in and that is the reason many of them never were able to go on to high school. They were expected to get jobs and share the financial burden.

Mom and Dad when they were first married during the Depression, 1932.

The jobs in Clinton were mostly centered around textile mills and so that is where my dad entered the workforce. The families that came over from Germany mostly had some type of trade experience and the Stoebel family was trained in the textile industry. So, it was inevitable that my dad would follow suit. As a point of interest, spelling of the family name in Germany was Stobel (with an umlaut over the Ö). But as my paternal grandparents entered the United States via Ellis Island, the name was changed to Stoebel because there were no umlauts on American typewriters.

Dad in his band uniform in front of the house he built circa 1942. He played the trumpet and would go on to teach my sister and me.

My mother, Flora Margaret Baer, was born January 1, 1907 in Clinton, Massachusetts. Her parents were also German immigrants from southern Germany near the Black Forest region. I remember her telling me that they were considered black Germans, not because of skin color, but rather that the political party in that part of Germany was near the Black Forest. I liken it to certain regions of the United States where the political affiliation is more likely to be Republican or Democrat.

Mom standing in front of the house she helped build circa 1942.

My mother's parents also came to central Massachusetts because of their expertise in the textile industry. In small towns across America, ethnic groups tended to cluster in certain areas of the town in much the same way they still do today. My parent's families gathered in the German part of town (Germantown) near the factories and the Nashua River. Other parts of town were predominately Irish or Polish or Italian. We were always led to believe that we wore the white hats and the rest of the town wore black, denoting, if you will, the good guys and the bad guys. That's just the way it was back then, but when I went away to college I found that was just small town thinking and all nationalities were pretty much the same.

My mother worked part time when I was young cleaning houses for local people and later worked in a pocketbook factory full time when my sister, Beverly, and I were in school.

Beverly (6 years old) and me (4 years old) on the front lawn of the home we were brought up in, circa 1948.

My mother was about ten years old when the USA got involved in World War I in 1917. Some of her brothers were already inducted into the Army and her eighteen-year-old brother (Edwin) was drafted for service. Some of the boys who served over in Europe were rotated back to the USA on leave and brought with them the Spanish influenza pandemic which affected hundreds of millions of people worldwide.

Edwin contracted the virus before he went overseas and died at home. My mom told me that he literally turned black when he passed and that is probably the reason you hear this epidemic called the black plague. No one went to funerals during that time because of fear of contracting the disease. There were plenty of horse drawn hearses going up and down the streets as my mother recalled. It was a devastating time in our history.

My parents met and got married when my dad was twenty-seven and my mom twenty-three. My dad played the trumpet in various bands and my mother spotted him playing at a town gazebo for a July 4th celebration. She thought he was a good-looking Italian guy with his thick, dark hair, but he turned out to be German just like her.

To spare the family the expense of a wedding, they eloped and got married by a minister in Beverly, Massachusetts. They lived in a third floor apartment in Germantown in a building that my maternal grandparents owned. This was in the 1930's during the Great Depression, so work was scarce. My dad did odd jobs on a farm and my mother would relocate weekly to Harvard, Massachusetts to work as a housekeeper at a well-to-do household. I remember my dad saying that he would tell everyone that he had been through Harvard but didn't divulge that it was not the prestigious University in Cambridge, Massachusetts! I always got a chuckle out of that.

As the depression era waned, jobs became more prevalent and my dad got back into one of the textile shops in town. I don't know where my mom worked during that period, but I'm sure they were both employed. They were saving their money to eventually move out of the third floor apartment they were renting and into a home of their own. My parents did not want to start a family until they were debt free and had their own home, so they saved for ten years before having children.

When they had scraped together enough money, they purchased a three-quarter acre piece of land which was part of a small farm at the east end of Clinton, Massachusetts on Chace Street. They were promised an adjoining lot as well, but as time went on that offer was withdrawn and eventually it was sold to another couple.

After savings were accumulated and my parents could afford it, a local farmer was hired to dig for the foundation. It was done with a team of horses. The topsoil was so good that the farmer scraped it all out of the way so as to not waste it and then dug further for the footings.

Because my parents were so resourceful and economical, they built the house themselves as they could afford to buy materials. My dad had a French carpenter help him with the framing which is at least a two-man job. Although there was a little bit of a communication problem, they got the job done masterfully. The Frenchman would call down to my dad… "Twelve feet, ten inches and two little black mark" which would be code for twelve feet, ten and one eighth inches. They obviously were able to work through the communication problem.

Later, my mom and dad worked side by side nailing roofing, siding, flooring, or whatever the task of the week was. Materials were hard to come by since this was at the beginning of World War II in 1940, so that delayed the project somewhat. The house was to become known as 344 Chace Street and is where my sister and I were brought up. The house and property were all paid for by the time they took occupancy.

Beverly Ann Stoebel was the first child born to my parents on April 1, 1942. She has been the source of all my April fools jokes since I can remember. She got the name Beverly from the town where our parents were married.

I was the next to be born December 27, 1944. I was supposed to be a Christmas baby. It didn't take long for me to figure out over the years that some Christmas presents were held back and repurposed as birthday gifts!

We had many happy childhood days at this home and my parents were wonderful, hardworking, Christian people who were making a good life for us all. Mom and dad spoke German at home when they did not want us kids to understand what they were saying. They did not speak it outside of the home because of the negative connotations of having just come out of the war with Germany. We were active in the German Congregational Church in town. The first service of the morning was in German and the later one was in English. As time went on and the older folks that came directly from Germany passed away, the service was reduced to just one English service with the occasional hymn sung in German. My dad was superintendent of the Sunday School for a while and my mother taught one of the children's classes. It was a wonderful time in our lives and life was good.

3. GROWING UP

G rowing up in the fifties was a nice time to be alive. We were after WWII and Vietnam had not yet become a reality. Living on Chace Street in Clinton, Massachusetts was as good a place as any, I suppose, for a kid to just be a kid.

We did not have the electronic devices that kids have today, so we made our own entertainment in the form of outdoor games and activities. Even though we lived on a street which could be considered a main artery, there was not much traffic. Back in the day, most families had only one car and that car would be used to commute to work or go for a Sunday drive. So, after the morning "rush" of only a few dozen cars, the streets would become one of our playground areas if we so chose.

On Sunday morning, however, I can remember one particular car rushing by the house at a pretty high rate of speed. I came to find out that it was Congressman Philip Philbin from the neighboring town of Bolton on his way to church over on what we called the "acre" part of Clinton and Saint Mary's Church. He would always attend this church when he was not in Washington, DC, and he was always late.

We pretty much all had bicycles, so that was part of our entertainment and exercise. My dad had told me that when he was a kid, he had a special trick that he would perform on his bike. While cruising along, he would put his feet up on the handlebars, scooch forward and sit on the handlebars as he coasted along. I decided to try that one day and so I got up to speed, put my feet up on the handlebars, and scooched forward to get my butt up on the bars. That lasted for only a moment—until the crash! Making contact with a hard surface with your butt is not the most pleasant feeling. Actually, it hurt like hell. Right then and there I made a decision not to try a stunt like that again.

I never really knew for sure if my dad ever completed that stunt successfully himself because he never divulged that to me! My butt still hurts to this day when I think about it.

One of the fun alterations we would make to our bikes back then was to take a playing card and affix it to the rear wheel strut with a clothes pin. As the card struck the wheel spokes in motion, it would make a flutter sound like a motor. We thought we were pretty cool. Does anyone still do that today?

I was riding my bike down a country road not too far from our house going trout fishing at a local stream. As I cruised along, I heard a sound above me. It was an airplane and I looked up to see it, only to become fixated on this beautiful flying object. I'm not sure how long I watched it, but it must have been just a little bit too long. Next thing I knew, I was going ass over teakettle into the bushes at the side of the road! I didn't know it then, but I would have a lifelong love of aviation from that moment on. To this day, every time an airplane flies over, I look up and gaze at it just like that day back in the fifties when I crashed my bike. Some things in life just never change.

There was an airport in Bolton, Massachusetts not too far from our house. The airport and surrounding land were eventually bought and turned into Suprenant Golf Course. I believe that it is now called the International Golf Course.

When the airport was still operating, my dad took me over there one time when I was probably six or seven years old. I can remember I was fascinated by all of the airplanes taking off and landing from the runway. Back then there were still plenty of biplanes in service, so we got to see them and the newer monoplanes flying overhead.

We had a neighbor down the street from us who, as a young man, was actively flying out of this local airport. He was certainly daring, as occasionally he would buzz his parent's house at very low altitude and come right over our house as well. I remember my dad commenting that he was going to hit our chimney because he was flying so low! The pilot of that aircraft went on to become a Navy pilot and make a career out of flying in the service of our country.

Watching and hearing the sounds of these low flying aircraft was music to my ears and further cemented the love of all things aeronautical in my mind. Aviation was going to be a part of my life. I knew it from an early age.

As a young kid, I loved to build things and automobile or airplane models were no exception. It seems I always had some sort of kit I was working on. I either bought them with some of my allowance or I got them as birthday or Christmas gifts. I spent countless hours in the basement where I set up a little hobby area.

As I got a little older, maybe ten or eleven years old, I progressed to gas powered airplanes which I and a buddy, Eric Schreiner, would fly in a circle in our back yard. It was called control line or U-control flying.

Using a U-shaped handle and two fifty-foot long wires connected to a bell crank on the airplane, the elevator could be manipulated up and down. The little Cox .049 engines ran on a nitromethane and castor oil fuel mixture at a very high rpm. After the engine was started, one kid held the airplane while the pilot ran to the center of the circle and picked up the U-control handle. When the signal was given, the helper released the airplane and, with a little up elevator, it leaped into the air to fly in a circle.

Eventually, we taught ourselves to not only fly in a circle, but to do maneuvers like wingovers, loops and inverted flight. Of course, there were crashes now and then, but that just meant going back to the hobby room to glue the pieces back together and prepare for a future flight. A bad crash was referred to as 'returning the plane to kit form!'

When a plane got really old, battered, and oil soaked, I remember putting a big firecracker in the cockpit with a long fuse, starting the engine, lighting the fuse, and taking off into the wild blue yonder. After a few laps around the circle, the firecracker exploded and blew the plane apart. Parts fluttered down in all directions. That was a big source of amusement and entertainment at the time. I think we were lucky that our folks did not know what we were up to and glad that we never got too seriously hurt doing these antics.

My dad complained to a neighbor one day that I was wasting a lot of money on the model airplane hobby. The neighbor remarked that it was not really a waste of money, but a learning experience that would become valuable later on in life. My dad concurred.

When I got a little older, I flew one of my planes at a local town sponsored event and won a trophy. I had hit the big time!

4. THE 1950s

Growing up in the early 1950's was certainly different from today. I remember when we got our first television set, an RCA console model with a black and white screen and a rabbit ear antenna. It had a CRT (cathode ray tube) and we were taught to never sit too close to the screen as the "rays" were bad for us. We got maybe three local channels and used various wrappings of tinfoil on the antenna to try to get clearer reception.

Years later, we had an antenna strapped to the chimney of our house to pull in even more channels (we then got six). In an attempt to have color television, my parents bought a plastic overlay that was taped to the screen. It was blue on the top, yellow in the middle and green on the bottom. Yes, we were really living in style with our "color" television. Eat your hearts out, neighbors!

During this time in my life I was introduced to scouting. I

began as a Cub Scout and my mother taught one of the Dens. I went on to become a Boy Scout and advanced to the rank of Life Scout. For some reason I never had the desire to make it all the way to the top rank of Eagle Scout. There were too many distractions with school and working on a farm after school. I was also a DeMolay boy which is a fraternal organization for young Christian men and a junior version of the Masons. I became an officer, requiring a lot of memorization for rituals and meetings. I think I participated in this organization for two or three years and then moved on.

On my twelfth birthday, I got the best present a kid could hope for. It was a J C Higgins .22 caliber bolt action rifle with a five round magazine and 4X scope purchased from the Sears Roebuck catalog. Most kids got a single shot rifle for their first gun, but I hit the big time with my five shot version!

I had my dad to thank for this gift because he was a hunter and wanted me to have the same experiences that he had in his early days. Of course, my mom had to buy in on a gift of this type also because she was the money manager and this was a pricey gift for its day. And, of course, there was the safety issue with a kid having a gun.

But, back then, parents spent time with their kids teaching them the difference between right and wrong and my parents were no exception. With many broken homes today and no father figure in the picture, kids don't have the opportunity to learn self-reliance and trust like we did back in the day. My dad spent time with me at the local rifle range teaching me to shoot properly and to handle a gun safely. I can remember my sister and I with my dad shooting at bottle caps as targets captured in the bark of a big, old maple tree. I never disappointed my folks and never got into trouble with the gun.

On occasion, I would take the rifle and walk to the armory in downtown Clinton. The military person in charge let me and my friends shoot in the basement range and even provided us with ammunition. Keep in mind, this armory was in the center of town and I walked there with gun in hand, no case, and no one thought the worse of it. If you tried to display a gun in public now like we did back then, somebody would call 911 and you'd be surrounded by SWAT teams, FBI, CIA, state police, local police, helicopters, and you name it. OMG, how times have changed! We have lost our innocence.

One of my first jobs when I was about fourteen years old was in an apple orchard in the neighboring town of Bolton. The job was obtained through a church friend who was the foreman of the operation. A retired Doctor Clemens owned the 150-acre orchard.

To earn a few bucks, kids picked "drops" which were any apples dropped by the pickers or those that fell naturally from the tree. The kids got fifteen cents a bushel and could earn a few dollars a day for our efforts. These apples were sent to the cider mill for processing.

My mother, who was the money manager of the household, allowed me to use some of the cash to spend (on model airplanes, no doubt) but the rest was put into a savings account at the Clinton Savings Bank in town for a 'rainy day.' I didn't know it then, but that money would help pay for my first semester of college. Mother was a smart lady who lived through the Great Depression and knew the meaning of saving a dollar.

The next year, I graduated to hand picking apples for twenty-five cents a bushel. I had hit the big time. But, I always longed to operate the farm machinery and eventually got to do that. I went from piecework to getting paid by the hour. I went from an hourly pay of $1.15 to $1.25 and made up to $70.00 in one week as a sixteen year old. I was in the big money now.

Since apple picking was seasonal, usually starting in August with early Macintosh variety and ending in late October with red delicious and golden delicious, I was lucky enough to work right through the winter months pruning trees and clearing brush. That first winter and spring, I contracted poison ivy and poison sumac from handling brush. Boy, was I a mess. The song "Gonna Need an Ocean of Calamine Lotion" was certainly true for me. The next season, I got a preventative shot from the doctor to ward off any effects of these outbreaks.

After pruning all winter and dragging the clippings to the rows in between the trees, a bulldozer with a big fabricated wooden rake on the front of it was used to push the brush to a clearing. The mountain of brush was then set on fire using old tires and gasoline to get, and keep, the brush pile burning. I'm not sure the method can be done in this day and age with all of the environmental problems which were not a concern back then.

Anyhow, this is about the time I learned how to drive tractors, trucks, and bulldozers as a fifteen-year-old. Even as an inexperienced kid, it didn't take long to figure out that you could get seriously hurt or even killed operating farm machinery.

I had some close calls with the old International W4

tractor and one of them was an incident of almost tipping over backwards. I was driving up a steep hill pulling a wagonload of apples and the wheels starting to lose traction. There are individual brakes for each main drive wheel, so if one of the wheels starts slipping you simply step on that brake and the other wheel continues to provide traction. But when both wheels are losing traction, the nose of the tractor starts coming off the ground. Houston, we have a problem!

As the slide backwards began, I hit the kill switch and steered the tractor back to the bottom of the hill without jackknifing. I was fortunate to walk away without any injuries. I was a lucky kid and I'm glad my parents never found out about it. Maybe it's a good thing that they never knew about incidents like this because they probably would have made me quit that farming job!

One of my fond memories was gassing up the tractor. In between the owner's house and the barn, there was an old gas pump, a crank type with a clear glass globe reservoir on top. You cranked the pump handle until five gallons appeared in the glass globe and you then dispensed the gas directly into the tractor tank. The amount of gas was recorded on a ledger hanging from the pump. I would love to have that old pump today as a collector's item!

Another job I had one day was to clear sticks and leaves off the roof of the owner's house. The slate roof was wet and slippery and I started to slide towards the edge of the steep roof. The more I tried to stop myself, the faster I slid on the wet tile. My only option at this point was to launch myself towards the nearest tree and hope for the best. I was able to grab the tree with my arms and escaped with only face and body scrapes. It is scary to think about what could have been a different outcome. Come to think of it, I was ahead of my time being an early "tree hugger", years before the term would be coined.

In summer, the new crop of apples must be sprayed to ward off the many different types of invasive bugs that can affect the quality of the finished product. One method of spraying was to use a "speed sprayer" that is pulled behind a tractor and blows the chemical laden water through trees on both sides of a row. Another method which was done from time to time, was hiring a local Agricultural pilot to spray from above.

One of the jobs I had, along with with the foreman's son, was to hold a pair of long poles with flags on the top to mark the rows of trees to be sprayed. The Ag pilot, with his Piper Pawnee, would then fly down the designated rows spraying at low level with his chemicals which probably included DDT, an insecticide known in later years to be toxic and have detrimental effects on humans. Of course we didn't know it at the time as some of the spray would inevitably settle on the flag pole holders and we were wearing no protective clothing or masks.

I was just thrilled to watch this Ag plane up close, clipping some of the tops of the apple trees with its landing gear and then pulling up to clear the large maple trees at the end of a row. It was pure aerobatic delight for me. I loved watching that pilot do his thing so low to the ground and I had a front row seat. This reminds me of a WWII pilot training sign that I saw one time about basic flying rules and it goes like this: "Try to stay in the middle of the air. Do not go near the edges of it. Edges of air can be recognized by the appearance of ground, buildings, water, and trees. It is much more difficult to fly there."

Sister Beverly and me in front of my first car, a 1950 Pontiac that I bought for $50 circa 1961.

Such was the life of this teenager with a part time job after school. Speaking of school, I was a pretty good student, albeit, a little lazy. School came easy to me, especially math. I got great grades through grammar (elementary) school and high school. Not top of the class grades mind you, but I was content with doing little or no homework and getting by with A's and B's. I wonder how well I might have done if I had really applied myself?

That was my personality and I was more interested in airplanes, cars, girls... anything but schoolwork. I took a driver education class in school and, just after I turned sixteen, got my driver's license. My dad had bought a brand new 1950 Pontiac years before and had just traded it in for a new Dodge at a local dealer in town. I ended up approaching that dealer and bought my dad's old car back for $50.00. I have many good memories of driving that car, taking girls to the local drive-in theater or just commuting to school and work. Life was good!

I would be remiss if I didn't mention somewhere along the way that my dad was a very good trumpet player. He was playing in several bands as a young man when he met my mother. She spotted the good-looking trumpet player at a local concert in the park one day and would go on to marry him.

Dad taught my sister, Beverly, and me how to read music and to play the trumpet. We played as a trio in church, in the school marching band, and in the school orchestra where my sister was featured in a duet. One Easter morning, we were to play at a church sunrise service. Because it was predicted to be a cold morning, dad lubricated the valves on our instruments with kerosene so that they would not freeze up. They froze up anyhow and we were not able to perform on cue. It was a little embarrassing at the time but looking back I can see the humor in it.

Dad was a very strict (German) teacher and at some point in my teenage years I had had enough of playing the trumpet. Beverly went on to play for a little while longer than me. I have my dad's favorite trumpet, case and mutes (conical inserts to alter sound) proudly on display in our house. I admire them, my dad and the memories of those days gone by.

5. HIGH SCHOOL

Having been born in late December, I was one of the youngest students in my Clinton High School class of 1962. I entered as a freshman when I was thirteen years old and graduated when I was seventeen and still wet behind the ears, as my dad would say.

Our school was located in the center of town across from the park which was, by small town standards, very big, very beautiful, and well maintained.

Statues commemorating war veterans were prominently displayed and there was a large fountain and wading pool where kids could cool off in the summertime. The old brick high school building was in character with the architecture of the town. It was spread out in two wings from the main entrance which was just around the corner from the police station.

During my sophomore year, the school caught on fire and was destroyed. Temporary classroom accommodations were provided at several elementary schools in the area and at the armory while a new high school was being built in another part of town. We would be the first class to graduate from the new school.

As the fire damaged building was being torn down a disassembled airplane was discovered in the attic. I am told that it was a Ryan PT22 or similar type of plane that was to be used as an aircraft workshop training tool. The airplane was eventually sold to a gentleman in the neighboring town of Bolton for pennies on the dollar and stored in pieces in a shed on his property. Every time I traveled past the shed, I remembered the plane and wondered what it would be like when restored. That old aircraft was stored there for an extended period of time and, over the years, many of the parts were stolen or deteriorated to a point where they were useless. What a tremendous loss of an historical aircraft.

Because we were sharing classrooms with elementary school kids, high school students went to school earlier in the morning… 7:00 a.m. as I recall, and we finished our day by 1:00 p.m. This gave me the rest of the day to work. I had been working in the apple orchard for several years by this time but decided to look elsewhere for a job closer to home and with higher wages. I got a job at a local printing company. I really didn't like the work and the smells of the printing operation, so I didn't work there for more than a few weeks.

One of the highlights I do remember was making a town dump garbage run in their old Ford station wagon that was powered by a flathead V8 engine. On the way back I ran out of gas so I walked the last quarter mile to the print shop.

The owner gave me a can of benzene and said: "Here, put this in the tank." So I trekked back to the wagon, emptied the contents of the can and started the engine. Wow, did the flathead like that high octane fuel. I think I could have won a race with the power that came out of that little V8 engine!

My next job was at the local Hamilton Hardware store in town. I worked there afternoons in my senior year and through the summer of 1962 until I headed off to college in the fall. The owners of the store were John Hamilton and his son Leland. Besides owning a successful business, John was on the board of trustees at the local Clinton Savings Bank and he was also involved with the Rotary Club in town.

Leland taught me how to play chess and invited me to join in with his chess club that got together from time to time. Bill Coulter was the owner of the *Clinton Daily Item* newspaper and one of the participants of the club along with other prominent businessmen in town. It was an honor to be in their presence and for them to accept me into the group. When I graduated from high school, John nominated me for a scholarship from the Rotary Club which I won and accepted at one of their meetings. The scholarship was for $250 and I really appreciated that.

Working at the hardware store was right up my alley. I was taught how to cut glass and remove and replace windows neatly with glazing putty. I was allowed to sharpen lawn mowers using a method that my dad had taught me and I waited on customers when I could. Of course, there were other duties like stocking shelves, taking inventory, and sweeping the store at the end of the day. Mr. Hamilton told me that I was the only employee that swept downhill towards the front of the store because there was a little tilt in that direction in this old building.

Mr. Hamilton drove a big, black Buick which he parked in the narrow alleyway behind the store. When he wanted to leave, he usually asked me to back the car out for him. Apparently he trusted me with this very expensive car. It's funny the things you remember when reminiscing about the past.

I was one of seven students in the class of 1962 that enrolled in the Technical program which was a step above general and college studies and consisted of higher math (calculus), physics and chemistry. I was also one of four students to be selected to the Boy's State program which was conducted at the University of Massachusetts in North Hampton. I don't think I was one of the smartest kids in the Technical program, but I made up for my shortcomings with hard work and determination. My class advisor did not recommend a big name college for me because of this.

He recommended Wentworth Institute in Boston which had an aircraft maintenance course that appealed to me. My parents wanted me to go to Atlantic Union College in the neighboring town of Lancaster, but the courses they offered were not to my liking. It was known to be more of a liberal arts kind of school. So, after graduation from high school, it was off to Boston for me. The big city would be a huge cultural change since I was brought up in a small town and accustomed to the surrounding country life. Bean Town, here I come!

6. BOSTON

In the fall of 1962, after working at the local hardware store for the summer, I was off to Boston to attend Wentworth Institute of Technology (WIT). I enrolled in the two-year Aircraft Maintenance (AM) class which would graduate in 1964.

I drove my 1950 Pontiac to Boston and parked in front of the dormitory where I would be staying. I had a small private room with a shared bathroom and shower down the hall. I met some nice guys at the dorm and in my class. This school was not coed at the time, so it was all guys. Most of them were my age but a few were just getting out of the military and taking advantage of the GI program.

One of the guys I hung out with was Toby Tomlinson from Burlington, Vermont. His father was a fixed base operator (FBO) at Burlington Airport, so he already had a lot of knowledge about airplanes and aircraft systems. Gary

Simmons from Martha's Vineyard was a pretty cool guy and I hung around with him from time to time. Frank Putnum and Lou Schaedler also became good friends and I stayed in touch with them after graduation.

Courses in the AM program were interesting. Besides studying the basic math and required elective courses, there were some hands-on ones that I really liked. There was a basic aircraft shop class for which we were issued a toolbox with wrenches, files, hammers, pliers, screwdrivers, etc. My name was painted on the toolbox and we took these tools with us when we graduated. I still have most of those tools to this day.

We learned how to do metal work by using hand tools only and we built a four foot section of a full-size airplane wing tip using the old dope and fabric method. After completing the wing and getting graded on it, the instructor took his knife and cut a slit in the fabric. I can't believe he did that after all of our hard work! The next project was to repair the damaged fabric and we were graded on that, too.

Shop also included engine work where we rebuilt an actual aircraft four cylinder engine. When the engine was completed, we mounted it on an outdoor test stand consisting of a metal shed with two engine mounts. Gas and oil tanks were on top of the shed with gauges and controls inside. One day we were running two engines at the same time and when we went to full power, the shed started to levitate and lift off the ground on the back side. We quickly shut down the engines and told the instructor about the incident. He said: "If you can get the shed airborne, I'll give you an A." Of course he was kidding... shop humor, I guess!

I was servicing the fuel and oil tanks on top of the engine test shed one day. When I jumped down using the motor mount as a hand hold, my high school class ring got caught on the mount and ripped my finger wide open. The finger became infected and I had to have the ring cut off because of the swelling. I learned a lesson the hard way that you should never wear jewelry around machinery. I still have a visible piece of metal in my finger that reminds me of the incident to this day.

We had a few full-size airplanes in the shop, one of which was an F-86 fighter jet. Our class president was kind of an obnoxious guy, so one day we got a chance to teach him a lesson. He had climbed up into the cockpit of the fighter jet to check it out and we took the opportunity to jump up on the wing, close the canopy, and lock him into the cockpit. We could hear his muffled calls to let him out, but we ignored them and left at the end of the shop session. The instructor found him some time later and helped him escape. The instructor must have thought it was funny because none of us ever got reprimanded for the incident.

Other shop classes included sand casting aluminum objects and a machine shop using lathes, drill presses and milling machines. I enjoyed making things with my hands and liked being around the machinery. I was definitely a hands-on type of person.

We also had two semesters of drafting. I was lucky

enough to have been given a very nice Henschel drafting tool set as a Christmas present from my Aunt Erna and Uncle Wally Ackerman. It was a German made set that I still have to this day. I used these tools for my drafting class even though I was issued another set by the school.

Does anyone remember what a slide rule is? We were issued a small Pickett slide rule to be used for quick and complex calculations. We did not have calculators or computers back in the early sixties so the slide rule was the tool of choice.

It was used for functions such as trigonometry, logarithms, exponents, multiplication, and division but typically not for addition and subtraction. I still have a couple of slide rules around the house someplace but I doubt if I could calculate anything on them now other than simple multiplication or division. Out of necessity, I was pretty good with one back in the day!

My second year at Wentworth went pretty well and I was getting good grades. I moved from the dorm to an apartment complex that the school owned. My sister, Beverly, and a girl friend at the time, accompanied me back to Boston to help me get settled into the apartment which I shared with a couple of other students.

I had sold my car and decided to use public transportation from this point forward until I graduated, got a job, and could afford another car. I did not know that women were not allowed in the apartment building but it was just my sister and a friend that were helping me carry belongings up to my room. A school appointed student monitor spotted us in the hallway and started to get really obnoxious about the girls being in the building. You know that phrase… "It's not what you say, but how you say it?" Well, this guy really pissed me off with his attitude, so I "escorted" him out of the room by his shirt collar.

Apparently, that didn't go over too well with the school because I was called to the dean's office the very next day. Long story short, I was put on probation for the semester and told that any more incidents like that and I would be kicked out of school. I behaved myself from that point on but I still didn't regret manhandling that peckerhead student monitor.

The apartment was just a place to sleep and study. My roommates were all good guys. The kitchen area was infested with roaches. If you got up during the night and turned on the light, they would all go scurrying for cover. When it snowed, we would take accumulated snow from the windowsills, make snowballs and bomb rats around the garbage cans three stories below. It was cheap entertainment.

One time we were at a party in another apartment complex near Fenway Park with some girls we met from Boston University. There was a commotion a few doors down the hall where another party was going on. We looked out into the hallway and spotted an obviously unwanted guy trying to get into that party. All of a sudden, a fist punched the guy in the nose three or four times and he dropped to the floor like a sack of shit. It was apparent he was not going to get into that party!

Later on in the evening, a knock came at our door, and when the door was answered there was a cop standing outside. As he looked into the apartment, it was very apparent that teenage drinking was going on in there but his comment was: "Wanna buy some tickets to the police ball?" Of course we would! We pooled what money we had and bought a couple of tickets from the cop and that was the end of that.

We had one student who was a really good guitar player. He was a very talented musician that could play any type of genre but was particularly good at rock and roll. He performed in a band for a couple of dances we had in the dormitory auditorium.

One night he was walking home with his guitar from a gig he had somewhere off campus. As he came through the park nearby, he was jumped by a gang of Boston thugs. They beat the crap out of him and stole his guitar. He somehow made it back to the dorm but was later admitted to the hospital with severe head trauma. His parents came to get him.

After some time, he came back to school, but you could tell that there was some kind of lingering brain damage and he would never be the same again. Sad case, but it just goes to show you have to be careful wherever you go and have situational awareness of your surroundings.

I remember watching the first USA appearance of The Beatles on the Ed Sullivan Show. It was on the television in the basement of our apartment building. Quite a historic moment and many students gathered around to watch.

I went on to graduate from WIT in the spring of 1964 with a certificate of completion in aircraft maintenance. This was not a degree program, although they did offer other courses where you could earn an associate degree. Years later, WIT would go on to offer full Bachelor of Science degrees.

I had an interview with a representative of Pratt & Whitney Aircraft during career day at school. They were located in East Hartford, Connecticut. I was offered a job as a mechanic in their experimental assembly and test department. I accepted the offer and I was off to begin my career at PWA.

7. PRATT 1964

Pratt & Whitney was the maker of jet engines for both
military and commercial customers. They were at one
time part of a bigger aeronautical conglomerate including
Boeing and United Airlines known as United Aircraft
Transport Corporation. In 1934, the federal government saw
this collection of companies as a monopoly and voted to
break them up into separate companies.

Pratt was the only remaining part that still called
itself United Aircraft until 1975 when it became United
Technologies Corporation (UTC). Under UTC were various
companies including Sikorsky, Hamilton Standard, Otis, and
Carrier. I did not know it back then, but I would end up
having a career working for Pratt which lasted for forty-
three years.

My first assignment was working as a mechanic in the
experimental assembly and test department. It was the first

job where I had to punch a time clock. I did not like that but reluctantly accepted the fact that this was part of working an hourly job for a big company.

The shop was not air conditioned and so I learned the meaning of "sweat shop" very quickly. I was assigned to work on military engines in the compressor module area. A lot of the workers came out of the military with experience in maintaining aircraft engines in the field. Here I was, a nineteen year old kid with no practical experience, working with older men (there were no women mechanics back then that I can recall), but they took me under their wing to get me started. The pay was pretty good so I was able to afford a brand new 1965 Ford Mustang. It had a V8 engine and four on the floor shifter. I thought I was hot stuff.

If you worked for Pratt, people referred to you as a "Pratt Rat" for some reason. The factory was an interesting place buzzing with activity. Big machine shops, casting and heat treat facilities, sheet metal shops, welding departments, experimental and production assembly areas, and test. All of this was spread out over acres of property.

The floors were made of wood blocks over concrete which were softer to walk on and, I suppose, would incur less damage if any parts were to fall on it. On occasion, during heavy rain, leaks dripping onto the wood block floors would swell the wood and sometimes create a hill several feet tall. I witnessed this many times in my tenure at Pratt.

There were air raid shelters in the basement since this was a defense facility and any assault on this country would probably target manufacturing businesses. During the Cold War with Russia this was always a threat.

Behind the factory buildings was an airfield. Rentschler Field was named after the founder of Pratt & Whitney, Fred Rentschler. It consisted of two main runways, a tower, and some outdoor test facilities. Pratt conducted flight testing out of this airport and also flew its corporate airplanes out of there.

Many years later, the land would be sold for commercial use. The University of Connecticut built a 40,000-seat football stadium on the former airfield and Cabela's sporting goods established a store on the property as well. I liked it when it was an airfield.

I had a couple of roommates at the apartment where I lived. They were both engineers. I'm not sure where I met Harlan and Ernie, but it was probably at an orientation class that we all had to attend as new hires. We had some good parties at that apartment and I can remember one particular Hallowe'en party that got a little wild.

Someone threw a pumpkin for whatever reason and it punched a huge hole in the wall. We hung a big picture over the damage until we could get some sheetrock and compound to patch it all up. We were on the second floor of the apartment building and the family downstairs was constantly banging on the ceiling with a broom handle to get us to quiet down. I'm sure they were happy when we were all off to work.

After less than a year working as a mechanic, I saw

a posting for an Engineering Aide job in the Mechanical Components group. I applied for the salary position and was accepted soon afterwards. It was a white-collar position so I had to wear a white shirt and tie to work every day. At least I didn't have to punch that stupid time clock anymore.

I was assigned to test various seal configurations under temperature and pressure conditions that the part would see in operation in an engine. I designed the rig to test these seals and had the parts machined in the experimental machine shop.

At that time, Pratt had extensive fabrication capabilities and made almost every part of an engine in-house. They employed up to 40,000 people at one time for the war effort in the 1940s. I was given a lot of freedom in my new job and so I spent time not only in the office but in the test area. My boss at the time was involved in some charitable organization. Another Engineering Aide and I were given the task of going door to door in neighboring towns soliciting donations for this charity… all on company time. I'm not sure how we got away with that, but the company never found out.

By this time, one of my roommates, Ernie, was getting married and moving out, so Harlan and I gave up the expensive apartment unit and moved into the first floor of a private home that was for rent. It wasn't long after that we realized the lady upstairs who rented to us had three daughters, all good-looking, Italian girls. We had hit the jackpot.

I'm not sure to this day why this lady would rent to two

young guys. Maybe she was looking to get her girls married off to someone with a good paying job. Regardless, things worked out well for us guys and I will spare you the details. Just use your imagination.

After working in the Engineering Department for a year, I came to realize that if I went back to school and earned a four year bachelor's degree, I could double my salary. I started to research various colleges that catered to the aircraft industry and came up with three of them that would accept most of my course credits from WIT. There was Embry Riddle in Florida, Parks Institute in Chicago, and Northrop Institute of Technology in Inglewood, California. I applied to all three. Northrop was the first to respond and, as it turns out, accepted the most credits.

My folks had helped me pay for my two years at WIT after my savings had been used up. I had not saved much money in the year and nine months that I worked at Pratt. I was just a foolish young kid who was spending his money on rent, car payments, and other expenses.

Again, my parents stepped up to the plate and said they would help pay for my education. With a couple of student loans and my parents help, I would be able to get an Engineering degree. My mother at the time was working at the Raytheon battery company in Clinton, Massachusetts and my dad was working at Colonial Press nearby (the textile industry had all but moved out of New England by this time and relocated either in the south or overseas).

My mother's earnings would be dedicated to my

education and they would live on my dad's paycheck. My parents even took over the payments of my car. I am eternally grateful to them for sacrificing so much to pay for all these things for my benefit. I was a lucky guy to have had such wonderful people behind my success. I couldn't have done it without them. I was off to California!

8. CALIFORNIA

I was accepted at Northrop Institute of Technology (NIT) in Inglewood, California and began my studies in the fall of 1966 in the Aircraft Maintenance Engineering program. NIT was started by its namesake aviation company to train airplane mechanics and technically educated people who were needed in the industry. The Institute evolved into a college that offered Bachelor of Science degrees in aeronautical, electrical and mechanical engineering.

I suppose, since I graduated from Wentworth (WIT) and would now be working on my BS degree from Northrop (NIT), I could be referred to as a NITWIT. I have been called worse, so I am okay with the moniker.

Inglewood was near the Los Angeles (LA) International airport. It was located just a few miles from the coastal beaches and not more than an hour drive from the foothills of the mountains surrounding the LA basin. The approach to one of the runways at LA International was almost directly over the campus.

When that runway was being used and an airplane approached for landing, it was so loud that our class professors would just stop midsentence, wait for the noise to abate, and then continue as if nothing occurred. That was normal operating procedure, given the location of the school, and we came to accept it.

I had a first cousin, Norma MacDonald, living in Palos Verdes Estates just south of the Los Angeles area. Norma and her husband Ray were more like an aunt and uncle to me. I was twenty years old at the time and they were in their fifties, so the age differential was why I looked up to them more as an aunt and uncle than as cousins. Their home was located on a hillside overlooking the Pacific Ocean and Catalina Island.

It was a beautiful place to live except for the fact that the whole hillside had been compromised by construction near the top of the slope. Blasting for a roadway apparently upset a subsurface fault resulting in the entire hillside slowly sliding towards the ocean. It was a slow-motion landslide, probably moving a couple of inches per month. But over the years it was devastating. Homes that were located near the ocean were destroyed or relocated by barge to another area.

US Route 1 along the coast had a noticeable jog in it which required constant maintenance to keep the road open. Water and sewer lines in the landslide area buckled and broke and had to be relocated above ground with expandable joints. I rode my motorcycle to the upper end of the hillside one day and viewed the gaping chasm along the fault line The gap was at least a hundred feet wide and probably as deep. It was an interesting geological phenomenon. This was California.

Norma and Ray helped me find a room in an apartment building near the Northrop campus. The school at the time had no dormitory, but they did help locate students into rentals in the area. I ended up with a couple of roommates from Hawaii to help share the rent. It was just a one bedroom apartment, but with bunk beds and a studio couch, it was enough to accommodate the three of us.

The complex consisted of twelve units on two levels with a couple of larger one level units near the pool. It was in a neighborhood of single family homes with an alleyway behind and some parking underneath the upper apartments. I lived with my Hawaiian roommates for a couple of semesters but then moved to a larger apartment with two different roommates, Bob and Steve.

To help defer the costs of my rent, I became the apartment manager. I collected the rent for our lady owner who lived over on the coast with her famous lawyer husband and young son. She apparently took a liking to me and trusted me to watch over the place. I reported any maintenance problems or late rent payments to her. It was a nice relationship.

For transportation to and from school and for travel down the coast to visit my 'aunt and uncle', I bought a small Honda motorcycle. At the time, it was all I could afford, but later on I sold it to another student and bought a Honda 305 Scrambler that had been stolen and repossessed by an insurance company. When I bought it, the motor was stuck but otherwise in good shape. So, somehow, I got it back to the apartment and started work on it.

Me and my Honda Scrambler in California circa 1967. It was a recovered stolen motorcycle that I rebuilt to running condition.

I tore the motor down and restored it to working order. I also painted the tank and fenders in a candy apple orange color which made the bike pretty attractive. Because this motorcycle was somewhat of a dirt bike, I used it not only for transportation, but for off-road riding in the hills of the Inglewood Oil Fields near Culver City. The hillside was dotted with oil pump jacks, something we don't see on the east coast.

Steve McQueen, the Hollywood actor, was known to

frequent these hills with his motorcycle as he was quite the daredevil and did a lot of risky stunts for the movies he was in. My roommate, Bob, went dirt bike riding with me on his motorcycle but he also owned a '57 Chevy convertible. Since my motorcycle was nicer than his (he had an old two cycle something or other) we would sometimes trade vehicles when I had a date or just needed a car. I'd get to drive his Chevy and he'd get my motorcycle.

The Chevy had a V8 motor and a three-speed manual transmission (stick shift on the floor) and I remember it used to pop out of second gear on occasion. Damn thing could break your wrist if you weren't aware of it. It was a nice arrangement for both of us. Bob was also the daredevil that did cannonball jumps off the second story roof of the apartment building into the pool that couldn't have been more than eight feet deep. We also had some great parties at this place. California girls, as I recall, were pretty hot. 'Nuff said.

We actually did some studying in between activities because, after all, we were there for the education. The college was on a quarterly system of semesters. Each semester consisted of about twelve weeks. I elected to carry a lot of credits and go right through the summer quarter as well. In doing so, I was able to graduate after seven semesters in the spring of 1967. I wasn't the greatest student, but managed to make it all the way through.

My other roommate, Steve, wasn't as fortunate. He was a nice guy but just did not have good study habits. He studied while listening to music which I could not do and which he apparently could not do either. At the time, Steve was also involved in restoring a WWII P40 Warhawk airplane at the March Field Air Museum in Riverside, California. I think he was more interested in doing that than obtaining a BS degree. Even though he flunked out of Northrop, he did go on to get the airplane into running and flying condition which was a massive accomplishment. I got my picture taken sitting in the cockpit of that plane when it was completed.

I was sitting at my desk at the apartment one afternoon working on my homework when all of a sudden the building started to shake. Books started to fall off the shelves and my chair started to bounce around as I sat there, dumbfounded. I was experiencing my first earthquake!

It quickly became apparent to me that no matter where you are when an earthquake strikes, you literally have no time to escape to a safer place. It was an experience I remember vividly to this day. It lasted for only a minute but it seemed longer than that.

Los Angeles is located on the San Andreas Fault and many people have speculated that one day this part of California will break off and fall into the ocean. I'll bet that some GOP politically oriented folks hope that will actually happen. Anyhow, that was the most severe quake I have ever experienced (I would guess 4.0 on the Richter scale) although I felt aftershocks from that one and some lesser quakes at other times while I was in California.

I started to take flying lessons at the local Hawthorne Airport while going to school. I think it was always a plan of mine to eventually get a pilot license. I paid for the lessons with money earned from odd jobs that my 'Aunt Norma' and the owner of the apartment building found for me. I painted houses, boats, and apartment interiors to earn the extra money it took to fly. Looking back on it, I kept pretty busy with school and my extracurricular activities all happening at once, plus studying for my private pilot exam. It was a wonderful time in my life.

Nearing graduation, I put out some feelers so that I would have a job waiting for me when I graduated. One of the contacts that I made through my aunt was a pilot out of Torrance Airport that had me fly the right seat while he practiced for his instrument rating under the "hood."

The hood is a device that one wears so that you can only view the instrument panel and not be able to see out of the windows of the plane in flight.

Through this contact person, I was able to get an interview and an offer from the FAA. I also contacted Pratt & Whitney and they flew me back to East Hartford for an interview with the Engineering Department. Pratt made me an offer with a starting salary of about $7,000.00 per year which was substantially more than the FAA at $5,500.00. What I didn't take into consideration at the time was that the FAA job came with so many more savings and retirement benefits.

I was eventually lured to Pratt because of the salary difference, which was more important to me than benefits at the time. Hell, I was young and I was going to live forever. Plus I would be back on the east coast and not too far from my parents in Massachusetts. And so, I accepted the job at Pratt in the JT9D Experimental test department.

My parents and sister flew out to LA for the graduation ceremony. They had never flown before, so this was a big deal for them. My sister had flown me back to Massachusetts for Christmas break the first year I was in California. I really appreciated her doing that for me.

The second Christmas, I drove back to New England with three other guys who were attending school at NIT. One of the guys had a Thunderbird and we all piled into it for the fifty-four hour ride from coast-to-coast. We only stopped for gas, food, and bathroom breaks.

I was so tired when we arrived that I think I slept for two days! Back in the 1960's, there weren't too many interstate highways and so we used part of the old 'mother road', Route 66, that took us through Arizona, New Mexico, Texas (those oil refineries smelled like really bad breath), Oklahoma (where we got stopped by a state trooper who just wanted to hassle us), Missouri, and up to Chicago. From there, it was due east to Massachusetts.

Looking back on this trip, I have a few memories that still stick in my mind to this day. While traveling a particularly long straight stretch of road through the Arizona desert, we blew the right rear tire as we were zipping along at one hundred miles per hour. After swerving off and onto the road a number of times to get back under control, we finally came to a stop. While changing the tire, one lug nut was frozen and we had to cold chisel it off. Other cars were coming past us at high speed and the wind shook our car which was up on a jack stand. Very unnerving.

In New Mexico at one of our pit stops, there was an Indian family that drove into the little town in an old pickup truck. The man and his dog were the lone occupants of the warm cabin while his wife and kids sat wrapped in blankets in the cold pickup bed. I guess we know who the head of this family was. The old, weathered Indian had his shit together!

After the holidays, it was just me and the owner of the T-Bird who drove back to California taking the southern route. We took turns driving while the other slept. I turned twenty-one on December 27, 1966 as we were approaching El Paso, Texas, so we stopped at a bar for a drink. There was not much going on there, so after my first legal drink we jumped back into the car and continued west. The girls weren't that good looking anyhow.

I suppose they would have looked better if we had continued drinking. Okay, I admit it. I'm a male chauvinist pig! I can accept that. We got back to LA safely and continued with our studies at Northrop. With graduation in the spring of 1967, it would be 'Goodbye California' and 'Hello Connecticut.'

9. FLYING

I knew when I was little that I would grow up and in some way be involved with the aircraft industry. I played with model airplanes and engines as a young kid, got my training as an aircraft mechanic, worked for Pratt & Whitney Aircraft engine company, and was now working on my bachelor's degree in aircraft maintenance engineering (BSAME) at Northrop Institute in California. I had always been crazy about airplanes, so why not complete the education process and learn how to fly? I was earning some extra dollars while going to school by painting boats, painting houses, and working as the manager of my apartment complex. School was going well and I had transportation with my motorcycle.

Hawthorne Airport was not that far away and there were a couple of aviation schools on the premises. I liked the people at Rose Aviation and signed up for flight lessons with them. My flight instructor was Dennis Crabtree. He was a very accomplished pilot and a great teacher, which I was thankful for. Dennis also loaned me his Jeppesen manuals to study for the ground school exam because he knew I could not afford to buy them.

My first flights were in a Cessna 140 which was a 'tail dragger,' meaning it had a main landing gear and a tail wheel. This was an older type of aircraft first manufactured after WWII in 1946. Over 7,000 of these airplanes were produced and Rose Aviation had two of them when I began taking lessons.

The airplane had dated avionics and I remember the radio was hand cranked to change frequencies when talking to ground control and air traffic control folks in the tower. Before starting the engine, a preflight check was always conducted. This consisted of a walk around the airplane looking at flight controls, kicking the tires, and checking for water in the gas. After preflight checks were completed, we climbed into the cockpit, buckled seat belts, called out CLEAR PROP, and started the engine.

Oil pressure is the first gauge that you check when the engine starts. Later in my flying career, I actually started an engine which had just been subjected to annual inspection. Something had been misassembled in the oil system resulting in no oil pressure. I immediately shut down the engine. If I had continued to run it, a very expensive aircraft engine would have been toast.

Because of the tail wheel landing gear configuration, it was hard to see over the nose of the plane when taxiing, so I learned the technique of using the rudder pedals to steer little left and right S turns, looking out the side windows and down the taxi way. At a designated location prior to takeoff, we pulled off the taxi way, turned the plane into the wind and checked several things. I learned a simple checklist that had been used on these old, fairly simple airplanes for years and it was CIGAR.

Controls—Move the stick or steering wheel full forward, full rearward, full left, full right. This check is to ensure that there is no binding in the elevator and aileron controls. Ditto the rudder pedals.

Instruments—check oil pressure, set altimeter to distance above sea level and check all other gauges to make sure they are in working order.

Gas—check fuel level of all tanks. They must be at least one quarter full for takeoff which I found out later in life was a vital step in the preflight checklist.

Attitude—adjust elevator trim to takeoff setting. This adjustment sets the elevator trim tab to a position which lightens the load on elevator controls and can be adjusted in flight for cruise and landing.

Run up—With brakes on and the airplane nosed into the wind, advance the throttle to takeoff setting, turn magneto switch from both, to left, to right and back to both. Watch for a slight drop in engine speed (Rotations per Minute or RPM). Pull carburetor heat knob and watch for a drop in rpm.

Most aircraft now have longer, more concise check lists, but this was adequate for the civilian aircraft of the time. Once given the clearance for takeoff, it was time to taxi out onto the active runway, line up on the centerline, and add full power. The steering wheel (or stick) was then pushed forward forcing the tail to come up.

Now you were able to see over the nose of the plane! Maintain directional control down the runway with the rudder pedals as airspeed built up (for this aircraft, a roaring sixty mph), apply a little back pressure on the stick and it was off into the wild blue yonder.

A Cessna 140 tail dragger like the one that I got my first seven hours of flight instruction in at Rose Aviation, Hawthorne, California.

I got my first seven hours of flight time in the Cessna 140. I learned takeoffs, landings, departure stalls, coordinated turns, radio etiquette, and emergency procedures. One of the first emergency procedures you learn is the dreaded "engine out."

Typically, flying along at a couple of thousand feet, the instructor would at some point discreetly reach down and turn the gas tank selector lever to "off" position. The engine quit soon thereafter and you immediately began looking for a safe place to land. Farmers' fields, highways or any relatively smooth place to set it down will do. You must demonstrate to the instructor that you have control of the aircraft, take notice of wind direction, and start to set up for an off airport landing if there is no airport in sight. The saying has always been 'A good landing is one you walk away from. A great landing is one where you can reuse the airplane.'

At some point the instructor (hopefully) turns the fuel lever back on and the engine should spring back to life. I knew another instructor who was doing this emergency procedure with a student. The engine coughed and did not restart! They hit the trees at the edge of a field and walked away from the crash with only some broken bones. They were lucky.

I arrived at the airport one day to find that both of the Cessna 140's had been damaged and were not available for training. A student pilot ran one of the airplanes off the end of a short runway and flipped the plane. Another student lost control with the other 140 on takeoff and ran over a runway light causing propeller and engine damage.

The only other training airplanes Rose Aviation had at the time were Cessna 150 tricycle landing gear models. These were newer aircraft which were manufactured starting in 1957. Over 23,000 of these aircraft would be produced in various configurations during the following years.

The tricycle configuration consisted of main landing

gear and a nose wheel so it was easy to see over the nose when taxiing. I thought to myself: "So there is a centerline down the middle of the taxi way after all." Transitioning into this aircraft was a piece of cake because it had modern avionics. No more coffee grinder radio. It was also much quieter and more powerful than the Cessna 140. This was going to be fun.

My next three training hours were in the Cessna 150. I was practicing takeoffs and landings with my instructor one particular day and, while taxiing back to the active runway to take off again, he said: "Pull over here." Dennis took my logbook and made an entry in it stating that I was cleared to solo. He then made a joking remark that he was scared to fly with me and was getting out of the airplane right there and then and I was on my own.

He opened the door, got out, smiled at me, and motioned for me to go. Because of the training I had received, I instinctively called the tower, got clearance to takeoff, taxied out to the runway, pushed the throttle forward, and went barreling down the runway. Before I knew it, I was airborne!

The airplane, being so much lighter without a second person in the cockpit, jumped off the ground... I was all alone. This is when the thought passes through your mind that you literally have your life in your own hands. It's not like driving a car or a boat solo for the first time. Trust me, flying your first solo in an airplane has a much higher intensity level.

So here I am climbing up to pattern altitude and turning

onto the downwind leg. All of a sudden, the tower calls me on the radio and says "Cessna 33 Sierra on downwind leg, we have an emergency. Make a right turn and enter into a holding pattern over Alondra Park at an altitude of 1,500 feet." Following instructions, I immediately banked right and headed south to the designated holding area. I could see my instructor growing smaller and smaller as I departed the airport airspace. He must have thought: "Where the hell is the kid going?"

A Cessna 152 airplane. I soloed in an earlier version of this type of airplane at Rose Aviation, Hawthorne, California after ten hours of total flight time.

I arrived at the holding area and started circling at 1,500 feet as directed. There were other planes doing the same thing but stacked at different altitudes. After fifteen or twenty minutes of circling (it felt like a much longer time), I called back to the tower and said: "Hawthorne tower, this is Cessna 33 Sierra and I'm on my first solo flight. When can you get me back into the pattern because my flight instructor will be worried about me."

The tower responded with a little chuckle, said the emergency had been cleared and I would be given priority to return to the airport now to set up for a landing. What a relief.

I turned back towards the airport, let down to pattern altitude, reentered the downwind leg, turned base, turned final, and made a perfect landing. I taxied over to my instructor and opened the door for him. He got in and I explained what had happened.

He was proud that the training he had drilled into my head had stuck with me and he was proud that I handled the emergency situation with ease. That was the end of flying for the day and an experience that I would remember for the rest of my life. Of course, when we got back to the hanger and parked the plane, I had to go through the time-honored ritual of having my shirt tails cut off. I also was presented with a nice award that commemorates the moment. I have this document framed and hanging in my man cave. The date was April 20th, 1967.

As my training continued, I did a cross-country trip with my instructor up to Bakersfield. This required Dennis to contact Los Angeles flight control because we would be flying through their controlled airspace. It was an overcast day, so I had to fly using instruments only as we ascended through the clouds. Dennis was instrument rated and handled the radio duties as I flew the aircraft, which was legal to do.

As we started to break through the cloud cover, I experienced a brightness that was beyond description.

I thought I had reached heaven. The sun was bouncing off all the water particles in the cloud and producing this extraordinarily bright effect. I did not have sunglasses on, but I looked over at my instructor who was wearing them and there were tears running down his face. This lasted for a few moments until we broke through the clouds and climbed into clear air. It was an experience that I had never seen (tearfully) before and I still remember the sensation to this day.

Our trip to Bakersfield was uneventful. There was beautiful countryside below us with vineyards that stretched for miles in every direction. It was a part of California that I had never seen before. After a stop at Bakersfield Airport, it was back into the air for the return trip to Hawthorne. Heading south, we were flying above the cloud cover and the smog in the LA basin.

On shore winds tend to keep smog and fog in the basin with the mountains as a backstop. Certain times of the year, usually October, high winds come from the west and blow all the cruddy air out to sea. These are called Santa Ana winds because they originate in the Santa Ana Canyon in Orange County. When I lived in southern California, I got my first look at the snowcapped mountains during these conditions which only lasted for a few days. As we cruised along at our predetermined altitude, the engine started to run rough. Typically, a rough running engine indicates carburetor ice, but how could that be happening on a beautiful day like this? We must have had the exact conditions of moisture and temperature because, with the application of carburetor heat, the problem cleared up and the engine started running smooth again. Just another data point on the learning curve.

As we approached Los Angeles airspace, my instructor contacted them and requested clearance. We were above the cloud cover again and I had control of the airplane. I flew our descent on instruments and the heading my instructor had given to me. Just as we broke out of the bottom of the cloud cover, I spotted a twin-engine airplane coming straight at us. We were on a collision course!

My instincts told me to haul back on the wheel to avoid the collision, so back up into the cloud we went. Dennis asked: "What the hell did you do that for?" When I explained what had just occurred, he complimented me on my piloting skill to react in that manner. Dennis had his 'head in the cockpit' and did not see the oncoming crisis. Add another experience on the learning curve!

That other pilot should have been 500 feet below the cloud cover and Los Angeles should have had both of us on their radar. Oh well, we lived to fly another day and I ended our cross-country trip with a 'squeaker' of a landing at Hawthorne. My first dual long cross-country flight was now in the logbook.

10. SOLO CROSS-COUNTRY

I was now cleared for my first solo cross-country, but, in the meantime, I flew with other pilots just to get some right seat time in my logbook. When flying an airplane, the pilot in command is usually in the left seat and can log time as PIC. If you are flying the right seat, you could either be an instructor or second in command which can be logged as such. I hooked up with another NIT student who already had his private pilot license. He asked me if I would like to split the cost of renting an airplane and help pay for gas. I agreed and off we went in a rented Cessna 150 out of Torrance.

Costs to rent an airplane back then were pretty reasonable. It was only $10 or $12 dollars an hour plus gas. Time was logged on a Hobbs meter and so you only paid for the time that the engine was actually running. We took off from Torrance and headed northeast over the San Gabriel Mountains. The mountains are almost 10,000 feet high in places and we struggled with our aircraft to clear them. On the Mohave Desert side of the mountains, we let down and landed at a small airport to take a bathroom break and gas up. This airport was used as a glider port because sailplanes were towed from there to fly along the mountain ridge slopes. Many altitude and endurance records have been set here because of the ideal conditions for slope soaring.

When we took off, we used the runway direction which would head us into the light wind. This was a single runway airport with no traffic control tower. As we started our takeoff roll, we noticed another airplane landing in the opposite direction, so we pulled back the power and stopped. I guess there were no rules at this small airport and the locals landed in either direction at their discretion. We finally took off when it looked safe and headed northeast again. You could see Edwards Air Force Base off to the right in the distance.

We were headed towards Lake Isabella and the small, old, gold mining town of Kernville. My PIC knew someone that lived there and was going to pay him a visit. I'm not sure to this day how he had come to know this individual, but he turned out to be an old, hermit like character. I was just along for the ride and to build some flight time in my logbook.

When we landed at the edge of Lake Isabella, the first couple of hundred feet of runway were underwater. They must have had a lot of rain recently. We powered the airplane over this stretch of runway and set it down where we found dry pavement. As we slowed down, tumbleweed was rolling across the runway and some of it bounced off the airplane. It was like we had gone back in time in the old west. This was 1967, but the rental cars they had at the airport were 1955 vintage and they only had a couple of them. So, we rented one of those old cars and headed up the road to 'the hermit's' place.' He was an interesting character as I remember. We had a light lunch, some conversation, and then headed back to the airport. After turning in our old rental car and gassing up the airplane, we headed back to the Los Angeles area.

As we approached the mountains, we climbed up and over the peaks at about 10,000 feet. This was pretty rugged terrain and you would not want to crash up in these mountains. My PIC had brought along a survival kit just in case. As we were letting down on the other side of the peaks we could see Los Angeles in the distance through the smog.

We got the bright idea to shut off the fuel, stop the engine, pull up the nose of the airplane to stop the propeller from spinning, set up a best glide path, and dead stick all the way back to Torrance. Seemed like a great idea because it was nice and quiet without the engine running and we would be saving money because the Hobbs meter would not be recording engine run time. We glided along like this for over half an hour and still had a couple of thousand feet of altitude remaining by the time we reached Torrance. The engine was restarted and we successfully landed a few minutes later. This was a great adventure that we had been on and I remember all the details of it to this day (except names of course).

My first solo cross-country was from Hawthorne down the coast to Lindbergh Field in San Diego. Lindbergh Airport was named after the famed aviator Charles Lindbergh who was the first person to fly from New York to Paris in 1927. His Ryan aircraft, *Spirit of St. Louis,* was built there in the San Diego area. After plotting my course, researching weather advisories and doing my wind calculations, I was on my way.

It was a beautiful, sunny day as I flew south along the coast at my predetermined altitude. Altitude is selected based on which direction you are flying. Because there is always a lot of air traffic along the coast, you obviously want to be flying at a different altitude than those airplanes coming at you. Flight altitudes in opposite directions are usually stacked 500 feet apart for small aircraft. So, for example, if your heading is due south you might select an altitude of 2,000 feet. Aircraft flying in a northerly direction would select 1,500 or 2,500 feet.

As I was cruising along enjoying the flight and the views, I spotted below me a bunch of landing craft with soldiers hitting the beach, military helicopters circling the area, and military vehicles all over the place. I was not warned about this in my preflight planning and was surprised to see this military action unfolding. I came to realize that this was training for the Marines at Camp Pendleton and did not affect my flight because it was all conducted at low altitude. Sure was fun to watch, though.

Now I had Lindbergh Field in sight and I contacted the tower for landing instructions. I was very cautious of this airfield because, not only light private aircraft fly into it, but commercial airlines fly into this field as well with big DC9s and 727s. It looked dangerous to me. Years later, in 1978, a private plane and a commercial airliner collided in the airport pattern. Everyone on both airplanes was killed.

As a student pilot, I was overly cautious and followed the air traffic controller's directions explicitly. Upon landing, I got my logbook signed to prove that I had been there and jumped in my plane to take off for the return to Hawthorne.

Taxiing out to the runway, I could see both large and small aircraft taking off or in the landing pattern. When I was given clearance to take off, I spotted a large airliner on final approach but still a few miles from the airport. I lined up on the runway centerline, advanced the throttle and began my takeoff roll. As I accelerated down the runway, the tower advised me to immediately make a right turn as soon as I lifted off to clear the runway for the 150 mph Boeing 727 that was fast approaching from behind. I did as instructed and got the hell out of the area.

Heading north at my assigned altitude, I was glad to be getting safely back to the Los Angeles area. It was an interesting and successful first solo cross-country flight that I was able to pen into my logbook.

11. BACK TO CONNECTICUT

After graduation from Northrop Institute of Technology with my BSAME degree in the spring of 1967, it was back to the east coast and, eventually, to my new job in the experimental engineering department of Pratt & Whitney. I had decided to take a couple of months off before reporting for work in East Hartford, Connecticut. I stayed at my parent's house in Clinton, Massachusetts and hung around the local Sterling Airport where I did some part-time work in the hanger and gassed airplanes.

I continued with my flight instruction and got checked out in the flight school's Cessna 150. It was now time for me to demonstrate my solo long cross-country flight which is a requirement for obtaining a private pilot license. I chose to fly from Sterling Airport to Portland, Maine and over to Laconia, New Hampshire as my three-leg cross-country.

After plotting my course, reviewing weather advisories

and preflight checking the airplane that I would use, I was on my way.

The first leg of the journey was the longest, to Portland. It was a nice spring day with clear skies and light winds. I left the central Massachusetts area and headed northeast, eventually entering southern New Hampshire and then southern Maine. I could see Portland in the distance. It was about this time that I felt the urge to urinate — okay, take a piss. I was still quite a ways from landing. What a dilemma!

I guess I shouldn't have had that second cup of coffee in the morning or, as an alternative, I should have brought a bottle to relieve myself in a situation like this. I would plan better for my next long-distance flights, but in the meantime all I could do was just suck it up, cross my legs, and get to Portland ASAP. I did finally make it into the pattern, landed and taxied over to the gas pumps. And, you guessed it. I rushed inside to find the nearest bathroom! Oh, what a relief.

After getting my logbook signed, it was off again to Laconia. This was the leg of the journey where I had to rely on instrument navigation. There were a lot of woods between Portland and Laconia and no visible roads, railroad tracks, lakes, or meaningful landmarks to use to navigate. They call this 'dead reckoning' navigation. I never liked that term because it had negative connotations.

And so, I used the radio navigation system to find my way to Laconia. It must have worked because before too long, I had the airport in sight. Success! Radio contact with the control tower gave me the active runway to land on and

I got into the pattern for approach and touchdown. At least I didn't have to take a piss on this leg of the cross-country flight. One of the local flight line attendants cheerfully signed my logbook and, after getting a bite to eat, it was off again to my home port at Sterling.

On my way back to Massachusetts I was feeling somewhat giddy since I was accomplishing my first long solo cross-country flight successfully, so I decided to buzz my parent's house. After a couple of low, low passes at the house, my parents and some neighbors came outside to watch. On my last low pass, I wagged the wings at them and headed back to Sterling. I hoped that no one took offense at my flying so low. All they had to do was get the airplane's N number and call the local police or FAA and I would be in trouble. The rule is that you cannot fly lower than 500 feet over populated areas. I was flying lower than one hundred feet. Foolish kid!

I landed back at Sterling and got my logbook signed. I was congratulated by the owner of the flight school and my instructor and since no one turned me in for buzzing my folk's house in Clinton, I was home free. I slept really well that night knowing that I had accomplished a successful long solo cross-country flight.

In the coming days and weeks of hanging around the airport, I fell in love with an airplane, if that is at all possible. One of the rental aircraft at the field was a 1946 J3C65 Piper Cub. It was a tail dragger. It had been used as a trainer aircraft at Fort Devens after WWII, then it was purchased by the flight school at Sterling. I just had to get checked out in it!

This airplane was a tandem two-seat configuration where the PIC sat in the rear and the passenger in the front. It had dual sticks for elevator and aileron control, no radio, no electrical system and no starter. To start the engine, it took two people, one in the cockpit at the controls and one in front of the airplane to hand "prop" the propeller.

It did not take long to learn how to prop an old airplane like this. You had to do it correctly or you could get hit by the propeller. Many accidents over the years were attributed to an error in doing this properly.

The PIC applies the brakes, turns the ignition switch on and yells: "Switch on." The prop guy puts his hands flat on the propeller blade (no fingers curled over the blade in case of kick back). He swings his right foot forward and pulls the propeller through compression as his right foot is swung back, thereby moving his body away from the propeller. This was a safe thing to do when choreographed properly and I went on to do this many times over the years. I even started an airplane by myself from behind the propeller with the tail wheel tied down, but that is a story for another day.

You have to give that propeller a lot of respect. I had a shop instructor at WIT that was working on an airplane one day. He rotated the propeller to give himself some room to work—and the engine coughed. That one rotation of the propeller was enough to shatter his arm and throw him about ten feet.

My first check flight in the Cub, N657M (November 657 Mike) was memorable. My instructor and I apparently did not prefight the airplane well enough because once we got into the air, smoke started to come from the engine and down the right side of the aircraft.

A Piper Cub coming in for a landing.

A quick pattern was flown to get back on the ground ASAP to troubleshoot the problem. It turned out that the oil cap was not properly fastened after checking the oil level on preflight. It wasn't me that checked that, it was my instructor.

Oh well, the cap was tightened, the engine restarted and off we went again for my first check ride. I never had a spin demonstrated in my flight training thus far, so we climbed up to 2,500 feet or so, reduced engine power to idle, pulled the nose up, stalled, applied full up elevator, and full right rudder. The nose dropped abruptly into a spin. If you have never experienced a spin in any kind of aircraft, you are in for a thrill. The maneuver scared the shit out of me the first time I experienced it (figuratively, not literally). The spin was taught at the time of my training but is no longer taught in utility class airplanes.

It is now considered aerobatic flight. It should be conducted in an aerobatic aircraft and with parachutes on the occupants. I read a saying from a Northrop test pilot that stated: "The Piper Cub is the safest airplane in the world; it can just barely kill you." There is a lot of wisdom in that statement. After some spin training, the real skill comes in recovery from the spin to a specific heading. I think these kinds of maneuvers made me a better pilot. In later years and with another flight instructor in the Hartford area, we did a spin from 5,000 feet in a Cessna 150 and started counting rotations until we had to recover. I think we got up to fourteen turns. What a thrill that was.

While working at the airport, I kept my eye on N657M. As it turned out, the flight school was thinking about selling it, partly because it was due for recovering the airplane fabric which is a major disassembly of the airplane. A Cub of this vintage had a chromoly steel tube framework covered by either grade A cotton or the newer fiberglass materials (like Ceconite) that were becoming available.

I jumped at the chance to own this particular airplane. The price was $1,500.00 and a bartered deal was struck for cash and work hours as payment. I used my 1965 Mustang as collateral for a $950.00 loan which satisfied the cash portion of the deal.

I now owned my own airplane that I could build flight hours with and fly whenever I wanted. I knew the fabric was getting old because one day I was washing the airplane and my hand ripped through the fabric in a couple of spots. That was not a good sign, but duct tape was used to cover the rips in the meantime until I could rebuild.

I flew my Cub every chance I could, weather permitting. One particular morning, I was recovering from a hangover due to a hanger party the night before. I decided to get a little stick time before I had to go to work. After takeoff and a few minutes into the flight, I realized this was not a good thing to be doing with my head pounding away from the hangover. I turned back toward the airport for a landing and commenced to bounce the airplane multiple times... really hard.

I was trying to do a full stall landing but flared a little too high. When the airplane stalled, it fell a few feet and bounced back into the air. I pushed forward on the stick to recover but that was the wrong thing to do. That action just accentuated the next bounce higher into the air. After the third bounce, I just pulled back on the stick for full up elevator and held it there. Final contact with the runway stuck and the airplane rolled only about twenty feet to a full stop. It was kind of a controlled crash landing. That was enough flying for the day and another data point in my learning to fly curve. DO NOT FLY WITH A HANGOVER! I tied the airplane down and went to find a cup of coffee and a couple of aspirin.

Speaking of crashes, I was working at Sterling one day when I saw a Cessna 150 come in for a rather awkward landing. The airplane was porpoising up and down just before making contact with the runway. After a couple of bounces, the nose gear collapsed, the propeller hit the runway, the plane flipped onto its back, and skidded down the runway to a stop.

I grabbed a fire extinguisher and took a hanger vehicle to the scene of the accident. When I got to the plane, it looked like the pilot was either knocked out or disoriented as he hung upside down from his seat belt. After opening the door, I was able to undo the pilot's seat belt and minimize the impact as he fell to the ceiling of the plane. By then, other bystanders arrived and helped to move the pilot away from the airplane in case the fuel leaking out of the tanks exploded.

The fire department and quick responders arrived on the scene moments later and tended to the pilot who survived with only bruises. The older gentleman was a student pilot who got rattled when he thought another aircraft was also on final approach. He panicked and forgot to fly the airplane. I witnessed other crashes and midair collisions in my career, some of them with a more devastating outcome.

12. ENGINEERING

It was now late summer of 1967 and I reported for my first day of work in the engineering department at Pratt & Whitney. I had basically taken the summer off after graduation from NIT and screwed around working part-time, flying my newly purchased airplane, and enjoying the break from my studies. Now it was time to get serious and buckle down to learn my new job as an engineer.

I did not want to go back into the Mechanical Components group where I worked as an engineering aide. I wanted to work on the actual engine. I was accepted into the JT9D Experimental Engine Test group which was developing the engine for the new commercial Boeing 747 airplane at the time. Only a few prototype engines had been built and were being tested in experimental test stands. It was a new, fledging program and I was excited to be a part of it.

My first job within the department was working with

High Pressure Turbine (HPT) blades and vanes. These blades and vanes operate in the hottest part of the engine just downstream of the burner section. The materials and technology to allow these parts to operate in this environment are critical and I would go on to learn all the proprietary secrets.

One of my fellow engineers took me under his wing and showed me around the assembly floor. His name was Lou Zimkiewicz. I didn't know it then, but we would become lifelong friends.

It was one thing to work for a small business like an apple orchard or a Hamilton Hardware store, but it was another thing altogether to work for a large company like Pratt. There was a chain of command that you had to adhere to, almost like being in the service I would assume. There is a saying: "Be careful of the toes you step on today because they might be connected to the ass you have to kiss tomorrow." That was certainly true in this large company.

Over the years I have seen many a career come to an end because of toe stepping and I was in it for the long run. I had to learn very quickly how to navigate the complex workings of a large organization such as this. I have seen absolutely brilliant engineers lose their job in a layoff simply because they could not get along with people.

After a week in the department learning the ropes, something was going to happen on this Monday morning that would change the course of my life forever. There was a secretary's desk not too far from mine that had not been occupied the previous week. The inhabitant of that workstation had been on vacation and was now approaching her desk. This young lady was an absolute knockout and I couldn't take my eyes off her. Her name was Brenda and she was built like a brick shithouse (I never knew why guys used that term, but it was definitely used for purposes like this).

I was going to have to get to know this girl as soon as I could muster up the courage. Over the next days and weeks, I worked on ways to impress her. She approached me later that first day and asked who I was and my response was: "What's it to you?"

Wrong, wrong, wrong. Why the hell did I say something like that to her? Not the way to impress a girl. I was definitely going to have to work on my style. Over the coming days, I approached her on numerous occasions to "borrow" things like a stapler, notebooks, pens, and folders. I don't think my strategy was working.

On one occasion, I left an envelope on her desk just for fun that read, "rattlesnake tails from Texas." I'm not sure where I had learned this trick but the contents of the small envelope held a paper clip that was bent into a U shape. Another paper clip was attached to a rubber band that was connected to the open ends of the U shape. That paper clip was then wound multiple turns and the assembly inserted into the envelope. When the envelope was opened, the paper clip would start to spin and it created a sound like a snake rattle. I thought it would be funny and a cute idea to get to know her better. Not. I was out of the office when the envelope was opened but I think I could hear her scream from the adjacent building. Yup, I'm gonna have to work on my approach to this sweet girl.

I got to know Brenda in the ensuing weeks and started dating her. Our first date was a trip to Bradley International Airport in Windsor Locks, Connecticut. I wanted to impress her, so I took her up to the control tower to watch the activity from this prospective. I don't think she was impressed, but it was an awkward attempt to introduce her to my world which was all about airplanes. We were spending more and more time together getting to know each other and that was my main objective.

Soon afterwards, Brenda reported that she would be out sick. As it turns out, she contracted a kidney ailment and would be out of work for nearly a week. This was my opportunity to win her heart, so I showed up at her house on Casco Street in Hartford almost daily to visit her. I brought flowers and other gifts to show my affection and I think it worked.

Brenda's mom and dad really liked me and had the coffee pot brewing for my daily visits because they believed that engineers drank a lot of coffee. They really didn't but it was a nice thought, nevertheless. Brenda's mom, Bridget, began inviting me over for dinner which was really nice since I normally ate at local burger joints… not the healthiest diet in the world.

I was 165 pounds when I graduated from high school and was still that weight when I began work for P&W. It didn't take long after meeting Brenda and her family that I started to put on weight because I was being treated to really good meals almost every night at their Casco Street home.

Brenda's father, Joe, was an interesting guy. He was born and brought up in a poor family in Manchester, New Hampshire. His given name was Alphie Adelard Gosselin and he was one of the youngest of ten children in the family. There was not much money for food or clothing. Joe's father worked out of town and was away almost all the time. The kids would steal or beg food just to survive.

At some point, Joe and a sibling were farmed out to a local monastery that took in children who came from struggling families. When I would have dinner with Brenda's family, Joe would eat more food than I could possibly take in and afterwards would exclaim "beautiful, just beautiful." He was appreciative of a good meal that he had been deprived of in his youth.

When Joe was about sixteen or seventeen, he lied about his age and joined the Army where he enlisted as Joseph Gosselin, so he could be referred to as just plain Joe.

He was stationed in Panama for a time where he went on to compete as a golden gloves boxer in the lightweight class. The man had no fear. He contracted malaria while on a twenty mile hike and was escorted back to the base by an officer on horseback who made Joe walk all the way. In the end, I think that this experience just made Joe tougher and I admired him all the more for it.

Within three months of meeting Brenda in that first awkward office moment, I asked her to marry me and offered her an engagement ring. I popped the question one evening at the cove in Old Wethersfield. She accepted. We would have to keep our engagement secret at work because, at the time, the company frowned on spouses working in the same department together.

It was a great time in our young lives and we kissed a lot. We didn't know it then, but we would go on to have two children and still be happily married after fifty years. Meeting and marrying Brenda was probably the best thing that ever happened in my life. She was a smart girl who knew the benefits of 'saving for a rainy day' and that trait would go on to serve us well in the years to come.

13. CUB

I was working full time at my Engineering job in Connecticut. The 1946 J3 Cub that I had purchased was up in Massachusetts at Sterling Airport. It needed to be taken apart and recovered. The "rag" on it would not pass muster in its annual inspection. A Maule punch device is used to test the strength of the fabric. If it does not pass this test, the airplane is considered not airworthy.

I didn't have to use the punch device because I had ripped the fabric by just washing the airplane. The duct tape covering those rips was another dead giveaway that it was time for new fabric. With the help of my neighbor and boyhood friend, Terry Lindsteadt, we removed the wings, struts and tail feathers at Sterling Airport where the plane was based.

Terry would go on to be the best man at our wedding some years later but I did not know that at the time.

I planned to recover the wings later at the airport, but I needed to get the fuselage to my parent's house in Clinton which was about fifteen miles away. Terry had a pickup truck, so we devised a way to tow it by securing the tail wheel into the bed of his truck and making the fuselage, essentially, a tag along trailer. We didn't have a license plate for the "trailer" so we just put a red flag on the propeller shaft.

To get from Sterling to Clinton, we had to go through the town of Lancaster. In this particular town there was a cop (Sergeant Pelki) who everyone was aware of because he was known to stop and ticket you for the slightest of driving infractions. Not much went on in this small college town (Atlantic Union College), so I assume he got his chuckles from stopping unwary folks passing through, not to mention collecting the fines that would justify his salary.

So, here we were in the pickup truck, towing an unregistered "trailer" through Lancaster at or below the speed limit. It's hard to overlook an airplane fuselage when you see one. I'm sure this sight had never been seen in town before so it didn't surprise us that we were now getting pulled over by Officer Pelki.

I suppose he could have written us up for a variety of infractions but he surprised us by being fascinated with what we were towing and the story behind it. We actually had a nice conversation by the side of the road and, after a while, he just let us go on our way with a reminder to obey the speed limit and have a nice day. Whew. We dodged a bullet that time!

Once the airplane fuselage was back at my parent's house, my dad was kind enough to let me take over the garage for the time that I needed to recover the fuselage. The first task was to remove the engine and gas tank which I stored in the basement. The engine was a four- cylinder Continental A65 which produced, you guessed it, a whopping sixty-five horsepower. It didn't weigh very much so Terry and I just carried it to the basement where it would lay until the fuselage was ready for it.

Cub fuselage ready for paint in the driveway of my parent's home, Clinton, Massachusetts circa 1968

Hell, the whole airplane only weighed 750 pounds. It was basically a kite with an engine. Work began by tearing off the old fabric and inspecting all of the weld joints for integrity and corrosion. When this was done, the fabric recovery process began. I chose to use Grade A cotton rather than Ceconite, mainly because of cost.

After the envelope was glued in place, it was shrunk tight by spraying with water. Once shrunk, the finishing process began using clear dope, silver dope (to reflect the sun's rays) and the top coats of Lock Haven Yellow. This color was the quintessential color for J3 Cubs. It is the only color that I think anyone should paint a Cub. I ended up with a fifteen coat (including clear and silver) finish that was wet sanded between coats. Boy, did that baby shine. And, of course, the finishing touches were the black lightning bolt stripe down the side that makes a Cub look like a Cub—and the bear cub decals on both sides of the vertical stabilizer.

Applying the famous Cub decal on the vertical stabilizer of my airplane fuselage.

With the fuselage complete, I installed the engine mount and the engine with the help of Terry. We pushed the completed fuselage out into my parent's back yard, put some gas in the tank, tied down the tail wheel, and started the engine to the delight of neighbors and passersby.

You don't see an airplane sans wings or tail feathers with its engine running in a residential back yard every day. Within a few days, Terry and I towed the completed "trailer" back to the airport. My dad could now have his garage back.

No stops in Lancaster this time. What's with that? How did we get through Lancaster without officer Pelki spotting us? Hmmm, he must have been on his lunch break or not on duty at the time so we were able to get back to the airport without incident.

Now it was time to concentrate on the wings which also had to be recovered. After stripping the wings of old fabric and inspecting spars, ribs, and fasteners, it was time to put on the covering using the same fifteen coat finish as on the fuselage. During this process, the fabric had to be sewn to the ribs.

The term "rib stitching" refers to the method which requires two people using a long needle to fasten the fabric to the ribs. The wing is suspended, leading edge down. The needle and special thread are poked through the fabric on the bottom side of the wing, through to the top side and back again to the bottom thereby capturing the rib. A special knot is tied on the bottom and the needle advanced along the rib a predetermined distance to puncture and repeat this procedure all over again.

All ribs need to be sewn like this for their entire length. Higher speed aircraft require closer stitching. It is a labor intensive process that has been repeated over and over again through the years on old planes like this. These days, wings are of different construction like riveted aluminum or composite materials, and for good reason. New materials are cheaper, stronger, and not as labor intensive.

Because I was now working in Connecticut, the airplane was a weekend project. I did bring some smaller parts back to Connecticut to work on them during the week and I recovered the rudder, horizontal stabilizer, and elevator components in my apartment in East Hartford. Neighbors, I am sure, got a whiff of butyrate dope from time to time drifting out of my room. Nobody ever complained. Maybe they liked the smell?

After all finishing was completed on the wings it was time to rejoin them with the fuselage. It didn't take long to install the struts and wings and now the Cub was starting to look like a real airplane again.

After completion, we pushed the airplane out of the hanger to a tie-down spot until I could prepare it for first flight. There it sat for the night. I got a call the next day that the Cub had been damaged and to come to the airport. When I got there and looked at my plane, it was heart breaking. It had bent left struts and the wing was drooped downward. This couldn't be good.

There was surely some internal damage that would have to be corrected before this plane could ever fly again. Speculation is that a low wing airplane had come in during the night and while taxiing to a tie spot near my plane, clipped the tie-down rope and broke the wing. I never found out who did it.

I did not have insurance on the Cub yet, so I would have to write it off as an uninsured loss on my income tax that year. It was back to the hanger for repairs.

After removal of the wings, I found the left front and rear Sitka spruce spars cracked. After studying my options, I decided to do a Reed Clipped Wing conversion so I purchased the STC (FAA approved certificate) to do the modification.

This conversion basically involves cutting three and a half feet off each inboard rib bay thereby shortening the wingspan by seven feet. This would save my spars instead of buying new ones. I also had to shorten both struts by cutting and welding them to fit (four big front struts are used).

The Reed clipped wing conversion increases the loads that the wings can take from a utility class of approximately plus or minus three G's (three times the force of gravity) to almost plus or minus six G's.) The airplane would now be more aerobatic. I suppose that I should have installed a larger engine, like a Continental 85 horsepower, but I was trying to save money and thought that I might hold off doing that until some time in the future.

During the repairs to the wings, my fiancée Brenda spent some time with me at the airport helping with the rib stitching. I think she found it interesting and I surely needed the help, so it was a mutual agreement to work on the wings together on weekends. We still talk about it today. I did scare her one time as she was pushing the big long needle back through to my side of the wing. As the needle "popped" through the fabric, I let out a scream and exclaimed: "You got me in the eye." I didn't hear the end of that clown act for a long time after.

14. WEDDING DATE

I had asked Brenda to marry me and we had a preliminary date in mind. Because I was still working on getting my Cub back into the air, that project was taking time and money that probably should have been devoted to our wedding plans. Brenda's mom, Bridget, wisely suggested that perhaps we should put off the wedding until I had completed the airplane. Hell, it was like having two loves at the same time... one was beckoning me to the airport and one was patiently waiting to get on with the rest of our lives.

During this time period, I was taking my final flying lessons in preparation for my private pilot license. I hooked up with a mechanic from Pratt who was also a flight instructor at the local Brainard Airport near Hartford. His name was Andy. I was training on a new Cessna 152 and also flying a rental Cub at Windham Airport in Willimantic. Andy was kind of a daredevil, so part of my instruction was learning how to spin the airplane.

Spins in a Cub are relatively flat and in slow motion, but a spin in a 152 was a little more violent with the nose pointed straight down. We also practiced wingovers and loops. Now, we weren't supposed to be doing aerobatic maneuvers in a utility class airplane and it sure would have been nice to have parachutes, just in case, but we did them anyhow. It was fun and it was a learning experience for me. I think it made me a better pilot.

Another fun thing that Andy devised was falling off a cloud. Let me explain. When I am in a tall building looking down at the ground, it is unsettling to me. But when I am in an airplane with no references, I am perfectly comfortable with the height. It is like looking at a real time map.

Now let me set the stage. We are flying on a beautiful sunny day with small, puffy clouds floating along at low altitude. We are on top of the clouds with our landing gear just dragging through the cotton balls. The airplane is slowed with throttle pulled back and flaps fully deployed. We are on the verge of stalling at a very slow speed. As we approach the edge of the cloud, the wheel is pushed forward for full down elevator and now we are "falling" over the edge of the cloud. The effect is like falling off a tall building. Let me tell you, that is a sensation that you have to see and feel to believe. Andy was laughing.

I had to remind myself of the old saying that "there are old pilots and there are bold pilots, but there are no old, bold pilots." I had to make sure I wouldn't fly beyond my capabilities, especially as a new pilot, but I was okay doing this maneuver with an experienced flight instructor.

If you fly long enough you are sure to have some memorable experiences. I have flown in marginal weather including wind, rain and show showers. I was never instrument rated (IFR) and flew under visual flight rules (VFR). VFR requires an overcast ceiling of no less than 1,000 feet and an estimated visual distance of three miles.

There have been times when I took off within VFR limits that later deteriorated to less than favorable conditions. Flying from Massachusetts to Connecticut one time, the ceiling lowered. I let down to about 500 feet and followed the highway below. The ceiling lifted as I approached Connecticut and I was relieved.

On windy days you can actually fly a small plane backwards. I've done this in my Cub and in a Cessna 152 with flaps full down into a 40-mph wind. Nose up, throttle back and the airplane slows to a crawl. All of a sudden you are flying backwards. How much fun is that?

Soon after my flight training had been completed, I made an appointment with the FAA instructor who would take me on my check ride for my private pilot license. Up to this point I had either flown with a training instructor, as a solo student or as a right seat pilot.

My FAA check ride began by plotting a course to a predetermined airport taking into account weather, winds, and altitude selection. After preflight of the aircraft, it was taxi to takeoff. I was the pilot in command, so to speak, and the FAA inspector would be watching my every move. As we got up to altitude and I set my predetermined course, everything was going as planned. I was in command.

Just then, the FAA instructor said: "I changed my mind, I want to go to so and so airport," which was not part of my plan, but it was part of his. At this point, under stress, I got my map out and plotted a new course and altitude to the new airport. I apparently did just fine because the next command was to put the hood on.

The hood is used so you can just look at instruments but not look outside the airplane. This test is intended to make you fly the airplane if, for instance, you were to enter cloud cover or fog and had to rely on instruments. Mr. FAA then took control of the plane and flew it into adverse attitudes to confuse the "seat of my pants." Hopefully you don't wet those pants while he is doing these maneuvers.

At some point he commands "your airplane." I scanned all of the important instruments like airspeed (are we going up or down), artificial horizon (are we turning left or right) and rpm (do we need to add or reduce power). After a few moments, I got the plane under control and back to level flight. I did it.

Now it was back to Brainard Field for some landings and takeoffs. The FAA inspector asked me to demonstrate a soft field landing on the grass runway parallel to the paved runway. I made the landing successfully but noticed that I had not used the carburetor heat control which is used every time you retard the throttle. The inspector said: "Nice landing." I said thank you and then admitted to him "and the next time I land, I'm going to use carburetor heat." He was very understanding and decided to overlook this error. It never happened again.

I went on to demonstrate a soft field takeoff and then greased my landing on the paved runway. My pilot skills must have been adequate because he signed my logbook and cleared me for getting my private pilot license. I had become one of only a few hundred thousand pilots in the USA at the time out of the millions of people that lived here. It was a grand accomplishment for me that I cherish to this day.

In the coming weeks and months, I was able to fly passengers now that I had my pilot license. On one occasion, Brenda went for a ride with me. We decided to fly down to the Connecticut and Rhode Island coast to do a little sightseeing.

It must have been cooler weather at the time because as I buzzed the coastline at low altitude, there was scarcely anyone on the beach. Brenda must have enjoyed it because she reached over to give me a big hug and a kiss. My reaction was... no, no, no, not now. At that moment we were barely fifty feet above the sand and surf and this required my utmost attention. I think she eventually understood the gravity of the situation and saved the hug and kiss until we got to higher altitude and on our way back to home base.

Another time, Brenda and I were just tooling around the Hartford area in a rented Cessna and I decided to surprise her by doing a stall. I'm not sure to this day why I decided to do this maneuver, but I'm still hearing about it fifty years later.

A stall is a simple maneuver that is learned during flight training. It is intended to show how the airplane reacts during a full stall landing. At altitude, the throttle is pulled back to idle (with carburetor heat on this time) and the nose of the airplane is gently raised by pulling back on the wheel or stick until full up elevator is obtained. As full up elevator is held, the airplane starts to shake which is an indication of impending stall.

Eventually the nose of the airplane drops as the wings can no longer provide lift. Doing this maneuver in a Cub gets a mild reaction when the nose drops. But doing it in a Cessna 152 is a little more, shall we say, violent. The surprise stall did not go over well with Brenda and to the best of my knowledge this is the last time she flew with me. In retrospect, I suppose I should have explained to her what I was proposing to do and allow her to opt out, but I did not. I've learned that she does not like surprises such as that.

I had a fellow engineer (Steve) who wanted to go flying in a Cub, but my airplane was not completed yet. We drove out to Windham Airport and rented their Cub. It was a windy day and probably near the limits of a light plane like the Cub. But we had a mission in mind.

I think we were going to meet someone at a neighboring airport. So, off we went with me as PIC in the front seat this time and Steve in the back. We landed on the designated runway and tried to turn around to taxi back to the hanger. The wind was so strong that I couldn't turn the plane around, even by applying full brake, rudder and power at the same time. We were a virtual weathervane aligned with the prevailing wind. Steve had to get out of the back seat, go back to the tail of the plane and help push us around so we could taxi downwind to the hanger. I then used the technique of taxiing downwind with full down elevator which held the tail down. With up elevator, the strong wind could flip the plane on its nose.

On the way back to Windham, I asked Steve if he would like to do a loop. He agreed, so I put the nose down to build up speed, pulled back on the stick, applied full power and went inverted into the loop. This is a positive G maneuver (no negative G forces). When I saw the inverted horizon, I pulled back on the power because speed builds up really quickly when the nose starts pointing down. We recovered from the first loop I decided to do another consecutive loop, adding power again as the nose came up through the horizon.

As we exited this second loop, I heard the sound of fabric ripping behind me and the elevator control became frozen. The rear seat in a Cub is a canvas sling with a couple of cushions thrown on it for comfort. The canvas ripped from Steve's weight and the G loading coming out of the loop and he was now sitting on the elevator bell crank preventing me from recovering from the loop. I yelled back to him to grab onto the back of my seat and lift his ass off it. This allowed me to recover from the loop.

We flew back to Windham with Steve hugging the back of my front seat and his butt hovering over his seat. This was another unique flying experience that I still think about to this day. I am thankful that we got back to the airport and landed safely. This reminds me of another saying that I had heard years ago: 'Mankind has a perfect record in aviation… we have never left one up there.'

15. FINISHING THE CUB

After repairs to the broken wing on N657M and modification to the Reed Clipped Wing configuration, it was time to test fly my rebuilt Cub. The airport manager sold me a refurbished Sensenich laminated wood propeller that fit the time period of this airplane and looked really good on the nose of the cub. After installing the propeller, gassing up the airplane and doing a preflight inspection, it was time for first flight.

This is the point in time where you start thinking of all the modification and assembly steps that you did and hope that you got it all right. Did I tighten the fasteners to the proper specifications or at least use German torque (GutenTight). Did I safety wire everything that should have been safety wired? Did I get all the cotter pins in place on critical components? No more delaying the first flight. I jumped into the rear seat (for weight and balance reasons) and buckled myself in. It was time to start the engine and taxi out to the runway.

After the checklist was completed (CIGAR) I lined up on the runway and advanced the throttle. Down the runway we went, me and my Cub, building up speed. Tail wheel up, sixty mph on the airspeed indicator, slight back pressure on the stick, and up, up and away. Everything was going according to plan as I climbed up to pattern altitude and turned downwind.

About this time, I was feeling some vibration that was not normal and it was starting to get worse. As I retarded throttle, the vibration decreased. As I increased throttle, the vibration increased. Something was not right. It was time to cut my landing approach short and make a quick return to the runway. I landed safely and taxied back to the hanger.

Post flight inspection revealed that the beautiful laminated wood propeller was starting to delaminate. It's a good thing I landed when I did because the problem could have morphed into a more serious situation. That propeller was removed and a metal one installed. Test flights after that were uneventful.

It was time to bring the Cub back to Connecticut, so I enlisted the aid of a friend I met through a Pratt contact. His name was Mike Metnoski. He also owned a Cub and kept it in a barn at his farm in Coventry.

Mike was an interesting character. He was the quintessential farmer with blue coverall jeans, a ruddy outdoor complexion, and some pieces of his fingers missing (which I find is pretty common among people who work with farm machinery). Mike let me fly his Cub occasionally while my airplane was being rebuilt. I took my future father-in-law, Joe, for a flight one day in Mike's airplane. Mike only had his student pilot license so he technically could not fly passengers.

His field was about 1,000 feet long with a ditch running diagonally across one end. Going in a westerly direction, the ditch was not a problem as long as you were airborne when you got to it. Taking off in an easterly direction was another story because it shortened the field to about 800 feet and there were tall maple trees at the end.

One hot, humid summer day we took off in an easterly direction with me as pilot in command and we barely cleared the trees at the end of the runway. On another occasion we took off in that same direction on a crisp fall day and cleared the trees by a hundred feet. Temperature, humidity, wind direction, and airport altitude all enter into the equation when planning a flight.

There were other times that I flew with Mike in his Cub. He put skis on it when there was snow on the field and we would take off and then do 'touch and goes' on Coventry Lake. I'm sure the lakefront owners and ice fishermen didn't take a liking to that.

Another student pilot by the name of Harold had an Aeronca Champ (fondly referred to as an air knocker) that he kept at a nearby airport. He flew into Mike's field to visit every now and then, but on one occasion an FAA helicopter was flying overhead and spotted the Champ sitting next to Mike's barn. They decided to land and investigate. Bad timing. When they realized that this plane was flown in there by an unauthorized student pilot, they grounded the airplane.

A licensed pilot had to fly it out of Mike's field. Harold got in touch with me and we arranged for me to fly his Champ over to Ellington Airport. I had never flown a Champ before, but what the heck, it was similar to a Cub except that you flew it solo from the front seat.

I checked myself out in the Champ starting with preflight and engine run up. When I was ready for takeoff, I advanced the throttle, built up speed, got airborne before the ditch, and cleared the trees at the end of the field. I pointed the nose at Ellington Airport.

As you approach Ellington from the south, you fly over corn fields at the end of the runway. On low final approach I had to keep advancing the throttle because the coolness of the corn was not providing any lift and I could feel the Champ getting sucked down into it. Once the corn rows had been cleared and the hot runway was under my wings, I had to quickly chop the throttle and shove the nose down as the Champ tried to balloon back into the air.

It is just one of those 'seat of the pants' things you do when you are flying a light aircraft like this. I finished the landing by squeaking the main wheels on to the pavement and rolled out to a complete stop. When I taxied to the fuel pumps and got out, someone complimented me on the landing. I told him it was my first time flying a Champ and I appreciated the compliment. Maybe I was getting the hang of this flying stuff.

The next week we flew Mike's Cub from his farm in Coventry to Sterling Airport in Massachusetts. There, I fired up N657M and we took off in our respective airplanes for the flight back to Connecticut. As we flew south at an altitude of about 1,500 feet, Mike's plane kept getting lower and lower in altitude. Did he have a problem? Was he going to have to set it down somewhere? We didn't have any radios, so I could not contact him. I was concerned. My concern was lifted when I realized he was just letting down to buzz a friend's farm that happened to be on our return course. It was a friendly gesture.

Mike climbed back up to my altitude and now we were approaching the point where he would peel off to return to his nearby farm and I would bank to the right to fly to Brainard Field in Hartford where I would be keeping my plane. I performed an instrument check which is a good thing to do periodically while in flight. I almost had a heart attack when I saw my gas gauge was almost on empty.

Did I have a gas leak? Was my engine going to quit? If I was leaking gas, would the plane catch on fire? Since we were closer to Coventry than Hartford, I turned in Mike's direction and followed him to Coventry for a quick landing at his field.

The twelve-gallon gas tank in a Cub is located behind the engine and up under the knees of any person sitting in the front cockpit. The gas gauge consists of a wire about fourteen inches long which protrudes through the gas tank cap. The wire has a cork attached to the bottom of it. When the gas tank is full, the wire is sticking up about a foot above the cap. When you don't see any wire, the gas tank is empty. Simple.

The problem in my situation was that the cork had come loose and slid up the wire creating the impression of an empty gas tank when in fact I still had plenty of fuel. I was lucky I did not have a more serious problem. Guess I'm going to have to fix that.

After taking off from Mike's field, I headed to Hartford and landed without further incident. I had rented a tie-down spot for the airplane, so I taxied to that location and secured the airplane for the night. I could not afford to rent an indoor storage "T" hanger, so I just took the cheapest option and tied it down outside. It was time to head back to my apartment in East Hartford. I had had enough excitement for one day.

Around this time I had spotted a 1960 Corvette convertible that caught my eye. It was powder blue with white side panels. I don't know what prompted me to even think of changing cars right now because I already owned a newer 1965 Mustang. Newer is better, they say, but when you are young, impulse seems to take over and common sense is not in the equation.

I went ahead and bought the 'Vette and sold the 'Stang to a private party. The 'Vette had a 283 cubic inch V8 engine and an automatic transmission. For some reason, and again on impulse, I decided to switch it over to a three speed manual transmission. A local shop performed the swap for me.

It was fun to go through the gears, like my Mustang and my Pontiac before that. Every piece of farm equipment that I had learned to drive on was standard shift and I had a stigma against automatic transmissions at the time. So now I was the proud owner of a Corvette and a J3 Cub airplane.

In my spare hours after work and on weekends, I spent time with my fiancée, Brenda. We could now plan our wedding date and decided on the spring of 1969, April 18th to be exact. The plans were in motion and I couldn't have been happier.

At Brenda's urging, we started a joint savings account which was difficult to obtain because we were not married yet and many banks turned us down. I'm not sure what their reasoning was but we did end up getting accepted at Connecticut National and started our savings account with $35.00. Now, some (not all) of the money I had been dumping into airplanes and cars would be building up a nest egg for us. There would be no more cashing my semimonthly check and walking around with a wad of money in my pocket. I was a changed man.

Occasionally I went to the airport, jumped in the Cub and went flying. Many people approached me for a ride in the Cub when I was at the gas pump. I made a couple of deals where they paid for the gas and I gave them a ride. It was like flying for free.

One day I got the bright idea to just screw around at

low level. Here goes that impulse thing again. I took off from Brainard and headed south to Wethersfield where there was a turf farm next to the Connecticut River. The spring freshet usually floods this area as snow melts and the river overflows its banks.

As I approached the area, I descended until I was below treetop level and maybe twenty or thirty feet above the ground. Flying like this is dangerous but I felt in control and always carried enough airspeed to pull up if I needed to clear an obstacle. I must have flown at this low level for fifteen or twenty minutes, wagging my wings at the occasional farmhand, dog walker or hiker.

I felt like a crop duster must feel, like when they were spraying the apple orchard that I used to work at as a kid. It was a euphoric sort of feeling, a feeling of freedom. And, I lived to tell about it. Then, it was back to the airport and back to reality.

I was performing 'touch and goes' at Brainard one weekend. When I finished flying for the day, I pulled up to the gas pumps to top off the tank before tying the airplane down. I noticed that there were a lot of people outside the hanger looking off to the east.

I was wondering what that was all about until someone approached me and said that two airplanes had collided and both of them crashed, one into the Connecticut River and one near the edge of the river. Apparently, both of them were approaching the airport from the same direction and one descended onto the other, probably in a blind spot. I couldn't help but think that one or both of those pilots had me in sight when the incident occurred and that was probably the last thing that they saw before hitting the ground. There were no survivors.

I was flying one day with a fellow engineer that I knew from work. His name was Russ Groff and he had some flying experience, so I sat in the front seat and he sat in back. It was a cold winter day and there was no heater in this airplane so we dressed for the occasion.

We took off from Brainard and just started flying in a southerly direction with no particular destination in mind. All of a sudden, I noticed gas dripping from the tank which was just above my knees and behind the instrument panel. It kept getting worse, so I turned back towards the airport for an emergency landing. The rear seam on the tank started to fail, probably from internal corrosion. I turned the controls over to Russ, took my gloves off and tried to stem the flow of gas by holding them against the tank.

This was not a good situation. We could turn into a fireball if a spark ignited the fuel that was dripping into the cockpit. We dove for the runway, got on the ground, got off at the first taxiway and shutdown the engine. It seemed like forever, but it probably took only five or ten minutes to get back on the ground.

Pushing the airplane back to the tie-down spot was embarrassing but certainly not as bad as catching fire while in flight. In the coming days, I removed the gas tank and replaced it. I should have listened to my dad when he suggested pressure testing the tank as I was rebuilding the airplane. Hindsight is 20/20. Another cliché is 'live and learn.' I'm just glad the lesson I learned was not a harsher one. We could have died.

16. GETTING MARRIED

B renda and I had set our wedding date for April 18, 1969. We were to get married at St. Augustine Church in Hartford which Brenda and her family attended. This was a Roman Catholic Church and I was brought up as a Protestant in a German Congregational Church. I had no problem being interviewed by a priest and agreed to have any children of ours brought up in the Roman Catholic faith.

I figured it was a good thing that our children learned about God and Christianity and it didn't matter to me which church provided the teaching. My parents, on the other hand, felt differently. When we announced our engagement to my parents, my mother started crying and ran into another room.

My parents were born and brought up in the small factory town of Clinton, Massachusetts and lived their entire lives in that town. Because of my German Protestant upbringing, they always hoped that I would marry a German Protestant girl. But what did I do? I gave my heart to a French Roman Catholic girl. Lord have mercy.

As time went on, my parents (especially my mom) gradually accepted Brenda and came to realize what a good person she really is. To appease my folks though, we asked the minister of my hometown church to take part in the wedding ceremony in Hartford. It was an ecumenical gesture to soften the blow to my folks. Our minister agreed to participate in the Friday night ceremony and the wedding went off without a hitch.

Brenda and I walking down the aisle after getting married at St. Augustine church in Hartford, Connecticut. April 18, 1969.

My best man was Terry Lindsteadt who was a good neighbor and boyhood friend. Our maid of honor was Gail O'bright who we maintain a friendship with to this day. My sister Beverly was one of the bridesmaids as well as Brenda's sister, Karen. Other family friends, relatives, and coworkers at the time filled out the attendees.

After the ceremony and reception, we were off on our honeymoon. It had rained for our wedding and it was still raining when we left the reception, but that didn't discourage us. I suppose everyone hopes and prays for a beautiful day for their wedding but we have heard that a rainy day is good luck. I didn't know that for sure, but we would certainly find out as we started our life together.

Our honeymoon was an interesting adventure because we were really just getting to know each other. Let's just say that it took a week or so to consummate our marriage. I respected Brenda during our engagement period and would continue to do so until we were comfortable being intimate with each other.

With no particular reservations having been made, we headed north to the ski areas in New Hampshire and stopped at one of the resorts in the White Mountains. It was springtime and the air was starting to warm. There was still plenty of snow on the ground so it was perfect for spring skiing. We rented ski equipment and spent a couple of days enjoying the atmosphere of this resort. During lunch on the resort patio, we had a breathtaking view of Mount Washington. Someone was passing binoculars around and we could see experienced skiers navigating the steep slopes of Tuckerman Ravine. Just a little too risky for us novice skiers.

Heading south the next day, we ended up in Boston for the night and had dinner in Chinatown. I think this was the night that Brenda changed her mind about marrying me and almost decided to leave. I'm still not sure to this day what that was all about, but in the end she did not leave and we were still together when we arrived back in East Hartford where we had rented an apartment.

The apartment was owned by a lady from Hartford that apparently had gotten a Federal Housing loan to buy the complex. It was "affordable housing" and our rent, set by the government, amounted to $114.78 per month. Other people we worked with were renting upscale apartments nearby for $300.00 or more, but Brenda, being the practical girl that she was, decided this was a good bang for the buck and we would be saving money for a house of our own.

Before we moved into this first floor apartment, the landlady reimbursed us for paint, so we scrubbed everything down and put fresh paint on the walls. The manager of the complex lived right across the hall. Doug and Betsy Pitkin took a liking to us and they were able to get us a new refrigerator which we appreciated.

One morning, Brenda decided to treat me to a nice breakfast of blueberry pancakes. She wanted to make the pancakes special so she really loaded them up with fresh blueberries, but not much pancake mix. They turned out to be these big blue blobs that I thought was hilarious.

Our kitchen door happened to be open and so was our neighbor's door. Right there and then I made one of my first big mistakes in married life as I said to our neighbor: "Hey Betsy, you gotta check this out" as I showed her the blue blobs. We laughed, but Brenda's feelings were hurt, and I realized I had made a big boo-boo. Suffice to say, I never got blueberry pancakes for breakfast ever again. Go figure.

The laundry room at this complex was in the basement at the other end of our units. To get there, we would go down the stairwell near our apartment and walk the dimly lit 200 feet or so to the washer and dryer area. One night I had the duty to go and wash some clothes. As I was nearing the laundry room, the lights went out. I heard the click of the switch and I could hear someone breathing on the stairwell.

This was not a good situation as I found out the next day. Someone on the stairwell had just broken into the machines to steal the money in the coin collection mechanisms. I started backing away in the dark, feeling my way back to our stairwell and safety. I didn't want to confront the thief under those circumstances.

I reported the incident to our manager but I'm not sure if they ever caught the thief. From now on, I would not let Brenda go into the basement by herself and I would only do the laundry during daylight hours.

While we were living in this apartment complex, we parked our cars just outside our bedroom window. We had the 1968 Firebird that Brenda had bought new just before we met and I had my 1960 Corvette nearby. During the night, someone had broken into the Firebird and stolen the eight track tape machine from the console.

This was the second time this had happened. The first time was in the parking garage at Hartford hospital.

We had just visited someone at the hospital and when we approached the car it was apparent that someone had forced their way into it and stolen the factory installed unit. We called the police to report the Hartford theft, but they were too busy to investigate thoroughly, although we felt that the perpetrators were still in the garage complex. I guess it was low priority for them and probably happened with regularity. So, after the second theft at our apartment, we decided to just repair the console and not install another eight track machine. You just can't have anything nice, it seems.

One morning, I was getting dressed for work and I happened to take one last look in the mirror before going out the door. I noticed something big, white, and fluffy on the back of my pants. What the hell is that?.

Turns out it was a rabbit cotton tail that my mother had given to Brenda. It was part of a Halloween costume that my mother had made for me when I was a little kid. Brenda thought it might be a cute trick to attach it to my pants for a good laugh. Hey, wait a minute. I almost walked out the door to work with that thing on my pants.

Can you imagine the embarrassment I would have faced walking into the office that morning? Brenda swears to this day that she would not have let me out the door with the bunny tail still attached, but I was never too sure about that. As a result of this incident, I developed a stigma and checked the back of my pants before leaving the house every day for years after that. Thanks Brenda.

We were getting comfortable in our life together as

newlyweds. After a couple of months of marriage, we decided to go on a vacation which was kind of like a second honeymoon. We would be much more relaxed this time around.

Atlantic City, New Jersey was our destination since we had never been there before and we heard that the Jersey shore was beautiful. There were no casinos in Atlantic City at that time, but the boardwalk and beach were the big attractions. It was an enjoyable time for us laying on the beach during the day and going to shows at night. One of the big piers had a pavilion at the outer end which featured nightly entertainment.

The opening show this particular night was a horse diving act which was a novelty to watch. The second show featured Tiny Tim who was popular at the time. He was a singer who performed on the *Tonight* show and *Laugh-In*. His signature song was *Tiptoe through the Tulips,* which he sang in a high-pitched voice. It was not very entertaining and the diving horse was a better act. We got up and walked out; it was that bad.

The next day found us at the Atlantic City Race Track. It was the one and only time we would ever go to a horse race. I bet $10 on a loser, but Brenda put $2 on Queen Louise to place—and place she did. She raked in about $65.00 which was a lot of money for the time. Go figure.

Later in the day, we rented a bicycle-built-for-two to cruise the boardwalk. As we peddled along, at some point I decided to take a turn and go down a set of stairs. Why you might ask? I don't know, I guess it was just impulse, but

Brenda was not too happy going along for the bumpy ride on the back of the bike. I heard about that for a long time afterwards. Dumb thing to do.

Another one of our little getaways was to Cape Cod. We spent our time on the beach and took a bike ride near Provincetown where we spotted a 1930s Bellanca airplane flying around. It was giving air tours of the area out of the P-Town Airport. I talked Brenda into taking a flight—to which she reluctantly agreed.

During our flight I struck up a conversation with the pilot and divulged that I had a clipped wing Piper Cub and did some aerobatics with it. That must have encouraged the pilot to do something a little out of the ordinary because on final approach he pulled the nose of the airplane up abruptly, almost stalled the aircraft, pushed the nose down, leveled out, and made a perfect wheel landing. He turned to me and said, "How'd you like that?" Of course I loved it, but Brenda not so much. Another dumb thing to do with my new bride.

After a year or so in our apartment in East Hartford, we began to look around for a house. We were living on my salary and saving Brenda's income for a rainy day. For some reason, we were looking for used houses in the Coventry area one day and happened to come across a new development in the Northfields section of town. We toured a model home that day. Most of the new homes were raised ranches which were a good bang for the buck because of their two-story construction.

They were building a particularly nice one which was slated to become the next model home. It would have an

A-frame style front elevation with stucco and Tudor beams. We had saved some money by that time and decided to purchase 38 Fieldstone Lane for the sum of $27,500. We had also gotten a credit of $500 for interior paint, which we would do ourselves.

Our first home, 38 Fieldstone Lane, Coventry, Connecticut in 1970.

With a short-term loan from our local East Hartford Credit Union and our savings, we put a $10,000 payment down and took out a twenty- year mortgage on the balance. In a few short months we would be able to move into our new home and get out of that low-income housing apartment in East Hartford.

When it came to closing day, there was still a list of things to be completed on the house. The lawyer who was representing us at the bank recommended that we not close that day which forced the builder to complete everything before the deal was consummated. The builder was known to have some Mafia connections and be a little shady in his dealings, so this was good advice from our lawyer. Years later, the builder went missing and it was rumored that he was taken out by the Mafia in a Jimmy Hoffa manner. They never found his body.

A few weeks later, we eventually closed on our first house and worked together to paint the interior. Brenda had never painted before, so when we were staining the backyard deck she ended up with paint running down her arms and dripping off of her elbows. It was a sight to behold and we still laugh about it all these years later. I never let her paint again after we completed that project.

17. FLIGHT TEST

We moved into our new house in Coventry that we had saved and worked for together. We were both still working at Pratt. Brenda voluntarily moved to another engineering group after we got married because, for some reason, the company frowned on spouses working together in the same group. They, however, did encourage spouses and family members to work at the company. Brenda's mom had worked there during WWII. She was like Rosie the Riveter. Brenda's dad worked there for forty years and so did some of her aunts and uncles. Collectively, they had a few hundred years of service at Pratt.

I was still flying my Cub on occasion when I could find the time. I was flying out over the Farmington River valley one particular day and I decided to see how high I could climb. The service ceiling for a Cub is advertised at 10,500 feet. With throttle advanced and a little up elevator,

I was only able to get up to 9,000 feet due to humidity and temperature conditions. Another factor might have been that I was gaining weight since I got married because of all the delicious home cooked meals I was eating. I had the nose up above the horizon but the Cub refused to go any higher. It was still pretty high altitude for a 65 horsepower airplane. Having had enough of this high altitude attempt, I stalled the plane and put her into a prolonged spin. I can't remember how many turns I did before pulling out, but it was a lot. It was my cheap thrill for the day. I turned back towards Hartford to land and tie down the Cub. I had to get to work. I was working second shift.

I was gaining experience in the JT9D experimental program but wanted to get involved with an actual engine. The JT9D-3 would be the launch engine for the new Boeing 747 airplane and I expressed a desire to get on a flight test program. Because of my flying interest, I was chosen as the second engineer on X495. This experimental engine would be the first to fly. The company had leased a B52 bomber from the government to use as a test aircraft.

This airplane would be based at Bradley International Airport in Windsor Locks, Connecticut in a special hanger. The airplane was so big that the tail stuck out beyond the hanger doors which were modified to close tightly around the fuselage. If you are not familiar with this airplane, the B52 had eight J57 P19 engines hung in pairs below the wings.

These engines were built by Ford under license from Pratt. Engines number One and Two were at the left wing outboard position, number Three and Four at left wing inboard, Five and Six at right wing inboard and Seven and Eight on the outboard right wing. Engines number Five and Six were removed from the plane along with the pylon that held them. A custom pylon was designed and fabricated to go in their place and X495 would now be hung in that location for flight test purposes.

Mounting X495 on B52 test aircraft. Me on the left (engineer) and a mechanic working out the details.

After the break-in of X495 at an experimental test stand in East Hartford, the engine was transported to Bradley for installation on the B52. The people associated with this program were the best of the best. From mechanics to engineers to flight test crew, they were all great to work with.

A Boeing test pilot and copilot were brought in for the initial flights and to train our pilots. The Boeing chief test pilot had been involved in an incident some years prior. They were performing high G load maneuvers in a B52 when the vertical stabilizer failed. The PIC considered ordering the crew to bail out, but they continued to fly the crippled airplane and successfully performed a risky landing.

These guys were pretty wild, probably because their job called for living on the edge most of the time. They arrived in the morning with panties hanging off the car antenna showing their conquests from the night before.

During high speed taxi tests, the Boeing test pilots got the airplane up to V1 (commit to fly) speed, chopped the engine power and stood on the brakes. This was a test for the anti-lock brakes. I witnessed a big puff of smoke from some of the tires the first time they did this. The anti-lock brakes failed on one pair of wheels, the wheels locked up and they smoked the tires.

These tires had metal chips impregnated in the rubber and had, as I recall, something like forty layers of belts. They scrubbed off most of the layers in just a few seconds. The antilock mechanism was then replaced for that set of wheels. First flights were successful and it was very evident how much cleaner burning the new JT9D engine was compared to the old J57's at takeoff.

The B52 was an interesting airplane in that the wings had to stay level during cross wind landings. To accomplish this, a calculation would determine how much the airplane had to be crabbed (nose to the left or right of the runway centerline) during takeoff and landing in cross wind conditions. The landing gear was then dialed in to line up with the runway. Wing tip landing gear assured that the airplane maintained a level attitude while in motion.

On takeoff, the rear of the airplane lifted into the air first giving a nose down appearance. A drag chute was deployed on landing and had to be repacked into the tail of the aircraft after each flight.

B52 test aircraft taking off from Bradley Field, Windsor Locks, Connecticut, 1968. First flight of JT9D-3 engine X495.

I felt honored to work on this program. It was fun for me and they were paying me to do it. I never was cleared to fly on this aircraft, but I spent many hours inside the airplane during ground testing and preparation for flight. For flight, the crew consisted of a pilot and copilot in the cockpit on the upper level and a navigator and a Pratt engineer on the lower level.

Ed Chappel was the Pratt engineer monitoring X495. Ed

would go on to be a good friend of mine until his untimely death from cancer many years later.

In a flight emergency if you had to bail out from the lower level, you ejected out of the bottom of the airplane. You could not do this if the landing gear was down. You would be impaled on the gear. The pilot and copilot ejected out the top of the airplane. There were stories circulating that military mechanics working on B52s in service and fooling around with the ejection seat controls, ejected themselves out of the airplane and into the roof of the hanger. The stories are probably true. Can you imagine that happening? Man, that would ruin your whole day.

One day I flew my Cub up to Bradley. I was working second shift and had the morning off. Since N657M didn't have a radio for communication with the Bradley tower, I gave them a call on the telephone and asked permission to fly into their controlled airspace. They readily agreed, gave me a runway assignment and told me to circle near the end of the runway at a predetermined altitude. I did that and when I was cleared to land, the tower flashed a green light in my direction.

I reduced altitude and lined up with the runway. Since the threshold of the runway was so long and the Cub could be landed in a short distance, I touched down and came to a stop short of where large commercial aircraft taxied on to the runway for takeoff. I taxied over to the B52 hanger and went in to visit the crew. Many admirers came out of the hanger to check out the Cub. It was a classic old airplane and everyone loved seeing them up close and personal.

When it came time to take off and head back to Brainard, I called the tower to ask for permission and instructions. They assigned me the huge taxiway near the hanger to use as a runway for takeoff. This would be something new, using a taxiway for takeoff. One of the mechanics spun the propeller to get my engine fired up, and I waved a thank you to him and some of the crew who were standing outside the hanger to watch my departure. I taxied to the taxiway, did my preflight run up and held for the green light signal from the tower. It was midday and the winds had begun to pick up unlike the calm conditions I had earlier that morning.

When I got the green light, I advanced the throttle to move forward into the wind and climb the crown of the taxiway. To do this, I had to use more power than usual and realized if I just went full throttle (balls to the wall) I could be in the air before I reached the middle of the taxiway. So that's what I did and the Cub jumped off the ground. I was now flying over the taxiway and gaining altitude for my return trip to Hartford. Talk about a high performance takeoff in my low performance airplane. That is part of the fun of flying a Cub. You literally have to fly it on the ground in high wind conditions. The flight back to Brainard was uneventful and that was my excitement for the day.

18. GRANVILLE

Most of my time working at P&W was either spent on the experimental assembly floor, experimental test or at Bradley Field. I was hardly ever at my desk. At the time, the head of the experimental machine shop was a gentleman by the name of Ed Granville.

Ed was one of the Granville Brothers who were famous for designing and building the Gee Bee Racer. They had a shop at an airport in Springfield, Massachusetts. Their Gee Bee Model R Super Sportster won the Thompson Trophy Race in 1932. It used a Pratt & Whitney R-1340 air cooled radial nine cylinder engine which produced a whopping 800 horsepower. The airplane was designed around the engine and had a top speed just under 300 mph.

When Ed applied for a job at Pratt, he flew a Granville Brothers built airplane into Rentschler Field which was behind the plant in East Hartford. I got chatting with him one day at work and he invited me into his office to talk business. His office walls were lined with memorabilia including, of course, pictures of Gee Bee aircraft.

The discussion eventually got around to airplanes and he found out that I owned and flew a Clipped Wing Cub. Ed had a Stinson Voyager at the time and it was based at a small private field in Somers, Connecticut. Ed had recently experienced a heart attack and could not pass his medical exam for solo flight but he still maintained his Stinson and flew when he could with other licensed pilot friends. He told me that if I was ever in the Somers area, to drop in for a visit.

GeeBee airplane built by the Granville Brothers for the 1932 Thompson Trophy Race.

One weekend, I was tooling around in the Cub and landed at Ellington Airport for a cup of coffee. When I departed, I flew over Somers and spotted Ed working on his Stinson at the private airport. I made a pass at the field to check it out and wagged my wings.

Ed waved and motioned for me to land, so I circled around, set up for a landing, slipped the plane to lose altitude after I passed over the large power lines at one end of the field and gently set N657M down on the grass landing strip. I taxied over to the Stinson and shut the engine down.

My Clipped Wing Piper Cub at a private airfield in Somers, Connecticut. Picture taken by Ed Granville.

Ed was happy to see me and we had a nice visit with a walk around his airplane and mine. Before I took off, Ed took a picture of me standing next to the Cub. He expertly propped my engine to get me started. He had probably done that hundreds of times before. I waved goodbye, taxied out to the end of the grass strip and took off. It was a beautiful day for flying and I was elated to spend time with this famous Granville brother.

Not too many days later, Ed spotted me on the experimental assembly floor and beckoned me to come into his office. He said: "I've got something for you." He presented me with a slide format picture of yours truly standing next to the Cub. I have taken that picture and produced multiple copies of it over the years. It is one of my favorite memories and I cherish it to this day.

Ed Granville was a true gentleman. Brenda got to meet him and his wife at their home in Ellington and she agreed that they were a truly lovely couple. It is amazing the people that come into your lives along the way and these folks were very special to us.

We had been living in Coventry for a few months at our new Tudor raised ranch. Since the house had been a model home for awhile, many people had toured it and had admired the style. We had some friends over and were relaxing in the sunken living room this particular weekend when all of a sudden the front door opened and in walked two couples — that we did not know.

They apparently thought the house was still a model home and just entered without knocking. When they realized that the house was now a private home, it was a very embarrassing moment for them. We all had a good laugh and left it at that. They apologized and left. It was an understandable mistake that we thought was pretty funny at the time.

We had the local Manchester Herald newspaper delivered to the door daily. It was a luxury that we afforded ourselves and it was a way to read what was going on in the local area. Our newspaper boy was pretty good about delivering on time and in all kinds of weather. When he came to collect, Brenda usually took care of that chore.

On one occasion, I happened to answer the door when collection time was due. As I paid him and gave him a good tip, he responded: "Thank you, sir." It was the first time anyone had called me sir and I seem to remember that it made me feel old. Heck, I was still just a kid myself at the tender age of twenty-six. I explained to him that I would prefer that he not call me "sir" anymore and I think that was the last time he did. "Sir," are you kidding me?.

Brenda had an uncle that lived nearby in Bolton. He dropped over to the new house on occasion to visit—unannounced. Ray was a nice guy. He worked at Pratt for many years and was a volunteer police officer for the town of Manchester.

One weekend, Brenda and I were feeling a little frisky. We started messing around in our family room on the lower level in front of a fire in our floor to ceiling fieldstone fireplace. One thing led to another and we made our way upstairs to the bedroom, leaving a trail of clothes in our wake. We made it to the master bedroom and continued with our love making.

Suddenly, we realized that someone had entered the lower level of our house and was making their way up the stairs. You gotta be kidding me. Who in their right mind would just walk into somebody's house without knocking? This surely was an invasion of privacy if ever there was one.

It turned out to be Uncle Ray and he did knock, but in

our passion we did not hear him and so he let himself in as he was accustomed to do. When Ray saw the trail of clothing going up the stairs, he must have realized what was going on and he retreated to the lower level.

I threw some clothes on and went downstairs to greet him. He had a big shit eating grin on his face and eventually, I guess I did too. What an embarrassing moment. We still laugh about it to this day.

It wasn't too long after that incident that Brenda approached me and said: "Ya know, you're pretty handy around the house and you're also pretty good at lovemaking, too, because I'm pregnant." What?? That darn thing actually works?

I was so thrilled at the news that I went door-to-door to all of our neighbors and let them know we were going to have a baby. This was certainly one of the life-changing moments in our marriage and we were now looking forward to our first child. Brenda continued working until it was obvious to everyone that she was pregnant. I'm not sure what the company policy was at the time, but I think they frowned on pregnant women working into late term. Brenda did work until just a few weeks prior to the expected date and was able to camouflage the "muffin in the oven" quite well.

The birth date apparently had been miscalculated because Brenda went beyond it by almost a month. Could this be the first ten month pregnancy on record? Should we contact Guinness? Then one evening the announcement came—"I've broken my water." Into the Firebird we went and it was off to the hospital in Manchester. Later that day our first child was born. It was a girl and we named her Kimberly Ann Stoebel. She was beautiful and healthy. This is what all couples hope and pray for.

Our family was growing and it was a wonderful time in our lives. Brenda stayed home to take care of our newborn child and I was now the sole provider for the family. This was getting serious and it was the time in my life when I realized that I was now responsible for more than just myself. I was responsible for my family.

19. EMERGENCY LANDING

We were getting our new house in Coventry finished off the way we wanted. The nursery for our newborn girl, Kimberly, was painted and decorated in girly colors and we were enjoying our new daughter. It was time to finish off the basement family room where we had a floor to ceiling raised hearth fireplace.

I wired the room for receptacles, lights, and TV connections. Walls were insulated and covered in sheetrock and paneling. I made a custom fieldstone seat around one of the lolly columns and we had the floor custom carpeted. The next project was a half bathroom in the laundry room which I did myself.

I was still flying, but not as much as before. Family and home took precedence. The rule of thumb was that a pilot should fly at least fifty hours per year to stay proficient. I was not, but that didn't stop me from flying occasionally either solo or with friends.

One of my former bosses at Pratt, Bill Staley, expressed an interest in doing some Cub flying on the weekend. Brenda said "go ahead" because she knew I loved to fly and needed the diversion from the stresses of work. I went down to Brainard Airport on Saturday morning, untied the Cub, preflighted, started the engine, and headed for the runway. After CIGAR, I advanced the throttle and took off for Skylark Airport in Warehouse Point, Connecticut where I would pick up Bill. I landed and Bill was waiting for me at the airport office. He jumped into the front seat, buckled up and we headed to the runway.

After we were in the air, we had no particular flight plan, so we just headed towards Simsbury Airport in East Granby and landed there for a cup of coffee. After coffee and a bathroom break, we jumped into the Cub and took off. On climb out, the engine coughed one time and then recovered. That had never happened before and I checked for carburetor ice just to make sure that was not the problem.

The engine ran smooth after that and so we made an excursion around Bradley International Airport, staying out of their controlled airspace. It was a beautiful morning for flying. I let Bill take the controls because he had some flight experience and I felt comfortable letting him fly the Cub. We eventually made our way back to Skylark, landed and taxied over to the gas pumps.

I was a little low on gas and estimated that I had about

a quarter of a tank remaining. They were out of gas at the pumps and they were not sure when the truck would get there to replenish the supply. After a while, I made the decision to take off and get back to Brainard. A quarter tank of gas would be more than enough to get me there and I could fill up the tank upon my arrival. I said goodbye to Bill and he spun the propeller to get the engine started. I taxied out to the active runway, advanced the throttle and accelerated down the runway.

For some reason I thought it would be fun to do a performance takeoff so when I was in the air, I held the nose down until the Cub built up some speed and then pulled back on the stick and climbed like an elevator. This was amusing for me and I'm sure Bill and any spectators enjoyed it too. It was fun for a moment until—the engine coughed again.

I immediately dropped the nose to maintain my airspeed and tried to make a shallow turn back to the runway. The engine quit. I leveled the wings and the engine started running again, so I continued straight ahead, looking for a place to land. Up ahead and to my right was a field. It was a turf farm and I would try to land there. As I approached the field off to my right, I started to make a shallow turn towards it and the engine quit again.

I put the nose down to maintain airspeed but I was headed for the trees at the edge of the field. I was going to crash into those trees and I braced for it. Just at that moment the engine started running again and it gave me just enough power and airspeed to pull the nose up, clear the trees and perform a dead stick landing in the field.

It must have been Divine intervention that gave me that extra burst of power to clear those trees and maybe it was a little bit of pilot skill to accomplish the emergency landing, but I do know that I was a lucky guy to have survived this incident. Remember, any landing you walk away from is a good landing.

I unbuckled my seat belt, climbed out of the Cub and started walking towards a nearby road. I got about fifty feet from the plane and my legs almost buckled underneath me. It was the realization of what had just taken place. I could have lost my life or been severely injured. I had a wife and daughter to take care of. Oh, what might have been.

It was then that I saw cars pulling up along the country road at the edge of the field. It was Bill and some other folks from the airport that came looking for me. They were happy to see me uninjured and in one piece. Hell, I was glad to be uninjured and in one piece, too.

By the time we got back to the airport, the fuel truck had arrived. If I had only been patient and waited a while, I could have topped off my tank and been back at Brainard tying down my plane by now. I still don't know to this day if the cause of the engine quitting was water in the fuel or just low fuel, but one of the mechanics brought some fuel back to the Cub, filled up the tank and ran the engine. Everything seemed okay, so one of the instructor pilots jumped in and flew the Cub back to Skylark.

In the coming weeks, the FAA got involved like they

do with any aircraft incident or accident. They found a few minor things on the Cub that had to be repaired or corrected (justifies their job). The Cub was good to go but it was at that point that I decided to sell N657M.

The combination of work and family pressures and the fact that I was not finding the time to fly enough to stay proficient as a pilot was more than enough to help me make the decision to sell. I got an offer from a local pilot and we finally agreed upon a price of $1,500.00 for N657M.

I look up the registration number from time to time to keep tabs on the Cub. It was subsequently sold to a fellow in North Carolina who owned it for a number of years. It is now in New Haven, Indiana and has a 95 horsepower engine in it according to the aircraft directory online. A clipped wing Cub deserves that kind of power for enhanced aerobatic performance. I have seen these vintage aircraft for sale for $50,000.00 or more and kind of wish I had held onto it. But that was then and this is now. It was the right decision to sell at that point in my life.

20. ENGINE TESTING

Working as an Engineer in the JT9D experimental engine program was a great experience. I was learning the internal workings of a high bypass ratio aircraft engine and getting assignments as the engineer on duty to monitor running engines in the test stands. A stewardess once explained to me that understanding how a jet engine worked was easy because they just go "suck, squeeze, bang, blow." She was almost right but it was much more complicated than that.

I really gained an appreciation for the complexity of these machines and the people who bring them to life. There are design engineers, performance engineers, structures engineers, materials engineers, aerodynamic engineers, statistics engineers, electrical engineers, test engineers, and many other engineering and support groups coordinating with each other to produce a product that will propel an airplane loaded with passengers into the air.

Many experimental engines are required in a program to test performance and endurance. There are even complete engines that are sacrificed for ingestion of water, ice, and birds. I have seen some interesting tests and test results over the years.

One such test for a high bypass ratio engine is the liberation of a fan blade at takeoff power to demonstrate that the blade can be contained. That is why, when an engine cowling is open, you can see Kevlar wrappings around the fan case. The intent of this wrapping is to keep a blade from exiting the engine and possibly piercing the fuselage of the airplane. This could be catastrophic and result in loss of life.

Bird ingestion testing is interesting to watch. A pneumatic cannon is set up in front of a running engine. A bunch of small birds (euthanized, of course) representing a flock are loaded into the breach and fired into the inlet. The engine must keep running at a predetermined thrust level for a specified period of time to pass the test. Similarly, large bird ingestion must also be demonstrated to the Federal Aviation Agency (FAA).

These birds are typically the size of Canada geese. During one such test when the big bird was fired into the inlet, the results were catastrophic, caused a lot of damage and the engine could not maintain power. Upon investigation, it was revealed that the big bird was still frozen when launched. There aren't too many frozen birds flying around in the sky and so the next test utilized a defrosted bird and the test was successful.

You have to be really careful around running jet engines and test stands in general. Sometimes the test engineer on duty has to go into a test stand while the engine is running at idle with the cowl doors open to check for leaks. I learned to lead with my hand out in front of me to test for the boundaries of hot or high velocity air that would be coming off the fan, bleed valves or exhaust.

Even at idle, the high velocity air can knock you off your feet and throw you down the exhaust ejector tube. I know one test stand operator, Warren, who was blown down the ejector tube but was able to crawl on his hands and knees back to safety. He became known as "tumbleweed." That same operator also burnt up an engine that had a fuel leak. He gained another moniker… "fireball." I have also witnessed the results of an engineer walking behind an engine after it was shut down, but still spooling down, and it burnt his hair to a frizz.

Besides the seriousness of the test engine business, there is always some humor that comes to mind. I was taking a break with the test stand operator and his crew one day in a basement locker and restroom area. Some of the guys were sitting around eating a sandwich or snack. In the middle of this space was a large wash basin where multiple people could wash their hands.

The wash basin was operated by a circular foot bar that you pressed to turn the water on which was dispensed from a circular ring above the basin. As we sat there, a new engineer that we had never seen before walked up to the basin, unzipped his pants and proceeded to take a whiz into the basin. We all looked at each other and burst out laughing. This guy was oblivious to what the basin was used for. The urinals and toilets were in the adjacent room. He had a lot to learn.

For some reason, I can still remember a scribbled statement on one of the restroom walls in that test stand. It read, "He who writes on shithouse walls, rolls his shit in little balls. He who reads these words of whit, eats those little balls of shit." It's funny the things you recall from the past. I'll probably teach my grandkids that little rhyme someday just for the fun of it.

One of our engine test stands was across Rentschler Field from the main plant complex. When covering the test stand during the day, we entered the airport through a gate and drove the perimeter road to the facility. During second and third shifts, we could either drive the perimeter road or, to save time, cut directly across the runway through a discreet opening in the fence.

One night on second shift, it was dark and I decided to use the short cut. The runway lights were off and the tower looked deserted. I arrived at the test stand and as I walked into the control room, the test stand operator had a phone in his hand and said: "It's for you." It was the airport control tower operator on the phone and he was not happy with me cutting across the active runway with my car.

On my way back to the office, I stopped at the control tower, climbed the stairs and begged forgiveness from the operator. He was actually pretty nice about it and explained that there was a protocol for crossing the runway and that I should have contacted him in advance. I departed the tower on good terms with him.

Fast forward to another runway crossing. I was making my last visit to the airport test stand on third shift. The tower was closed, so it was safe to cross the runway. But there was another dilemma. Fog. The morning fog was so thick that I couldn't see a foot in front of my car, whether the lights were on or off. It had to have been an hour that I was lost out there, inching along and finding one dead end after another, until I finally found the opening in the perimeter fence. That was a scary experience and I'm glad I didn't get caught out there on that runway again. It would have been hell to pay.

Our engineering group needed a volunteer to go to Florida. Pratt had a military assembly and test facility in West Palm Beach (WPB) out on the Beeline Highway near Indiantown. Our commercial engine group had built a couple of outdoor test stands there to test the JT9D engine. C10 test stand was running an endurance program on one of our engines. Our young daughter, Kimberly, was approaching two years old at the time and I asked my wife, Brenda, if she would like to go with me for a six month tour. She agreed and so I volunteered for the program.

The company would pay for my flight down to WPB, food allowance, a rental car and a nice motel for the duration. They would not pay for Brenda or Kimberly's flight but would pay me the equivalent cost of my flight if I elected to drive there. We took the driving option which would more than compensate us for gas and lodging.

So, the three of us went off in our Ford Pinto hatchback. Our daughter was plunked in the back somewhere with the luggage. We found out years later that the Ford Pinto had a hazardous condition that was involved in a recall. If you happened to get hit hard enough in the back bumper, the gas tank could be shoved into the rear end and explode. We did not know this at the time. Ignorance is bliss.

We arrived in the Daytona Beach area in late afternoon and thought it would be fun to drive on the beach. Heck, they used to race cars there back in the day. We did drive on the beach, but when we stopped and opened the door to stretch our legs, out daughter tumbled out on to the sand.

It was funny at the time but she remarks to this day that we should have left her there. She said she would have made a great Florida girl, warm air, sunshine, horses. It just didn't work out that way but I'll bet she will someday be back in Florida to make it her home state.

After a brief stay on the beach, it was off to WPB which was still some four hours further south. Florida is a big state and we arrived at our motel destination that night in the pouring rain. We actually had to follow the taillights of a tractor trailer down the highway because it was raining so hard.

We stayed at 'Tahiti on the Ocean' on Singer Island which turned out to be a wonderful motel. It had two pools, barbecue grills, putt-putt golf and it was right on a sandy beach. What a great place it was for Brenda and Kimberly to hang out while I was at work. The next day we rented a car which was provided for us. It was a brand new Oldsmobile Cutlass Supreme. I used the Pinto for work and Brenda had the use of the Olds for her excursions during the day. This was going to be a great adventure for all of us.

21. TEST STAND C10

The test area where I would be spending my working hours was located about twenty-five miles from Singer Island. The commute didn't take much more than a half hour since I could drive really fast on the Bee Line Highway. The Bee Line was a straight, two lane road that went from the coastal area to Indiantown near Lake Okeechobee. The Pratt & Whitney facility was located along this stretch of road and at the edge of the Everglades Wildlife area. In other words... swamp.

After entering the property and going through the security checkpoint, I drove past the private airport that Pratt owned and operated and on down a long road to the test area. After parking the car and going through another security shack, I made my way to the test stand at the back edge of the property. I met with the engineer, Hank, that I was going to replace and he introduced me to the first shift test stand crew I'd be working with. Our test engine was part way through an endurance test but was shut down at the time I arrived. The control room was an air-conditioned blockhouse remotely located from the engine. The engine was positioned about one hundred feet away in an outdoor test stand.

We walked out to the engine which was suspended above us. To work on the engine, a truck with a raised platform was backed up and situated just underneath it. It was a crude but adequate way to access the engine for maintenance. The truck platform was removed when the engine was started.

Hank headed back to East Hartford and I was now the engineer in charge of the C10 endurance program. In the coming days I would find myself getting comfortable with my new surroundings. I reported to my boss up north by phone on a daily basis , but I was basically on my own to run the program. My first and second shift crews were great and easy to get along with.

I knew they were getting used to me too because one morning when I arrived for work, we said our "good mornings" and I opened my briefcase which I usually left on the engineer's desk overnight. To my surprise as I lifted the lid, there was a snake in the case. Holy shit, I hate snakes, even dead snakes. They had affixed the head of the snake to the lid of the briefcase and as I lifted it, the movement startled me.

I slammed the lid shut and told them I was going for a cup of coffee. "When I come back, that God damned snake better be gone." Perhaps it was a half hour later when I came back with my coffee. The snake was gone and we all had a good laugh about it. I'm thinking this is the way guys are supposed to bond? Maybe it was a rite of passage? For some reason I don't think women would do it the same way, though.

Because I had a first and second shift crew, I stayed most days to get the evening crew on task, whether it was running the engine or doing maintenance on it. Sometimes I had to come back to the test area in the evening if there was a problem I could not solve over the phone.

One particular night I was leaving the test stand. There were some dark areas between buildings as I made my way to the car in the parking lot. At night, snakes were known to be prowling around in the dark to lay on the warm pavement that had been heated during the day by the intense Florida sunshine. On this night I happened to step on a snake. I must have jumped five feet in the air and it felt like I didn't come down until I reached the car. Damn, I hate snakes.

My fear was tempered the next morning when I came into work. I retraced my steps from the night before and realized there was a rubber hose stretched across the path where I had stepped on 'the snake.' It still scared the shit out of me as I recalled the incident. I'm going to have to be more careful from now on. Situational awareness is what it is called.

I wasn't the only one to step on a snake. I never saw a full-size rattlesnake while I was there, but I knew they existed. One of the test stand crew told me of an incident where he was hunting nearby one day. They had a jacked up jeep that they sat on as they drove through the swamp and palmetto bushes. They had a couple of rear seats that were intentionally raised and this is where they sat with their shotguns at the ready.

Their hunting dog was working the brush in front of them to flush birds like quail and ruffed grouse. All of a sudden, this huge rattlesnake struck at the dog and bit him in the neck. My friend said it sounded like the dog got hit with a two-by-four from the impact. They killed the snake and got the dog to a vet as soon as they could, but the dog died from the bite. Sad story.

There were a lot of snakes around the test area but the only kind of poisonous snakes I saw were water moccasins (also called cotton mouth because of the white inside their mouth) and pygmy rattlesnakes. Pygmy rattlesnakes are smaller than their big counterparts, but still venomous.

One night a test stand crew member was exiting the blockhouse to go to the bathroom in an adjacent building. When he stepped outside, there was a pigmy rattlesnake warming itself on the pavement. It struck at him. After jumping up and down a few times to avoid getting bit, he finally came down on the head, killing the snake. The morning crew had the evidence still laying outside the control room for me to see when I arrived. Thanks, guys, at least it was not in my briefcase this time.

One evening we were out working on the engine doing some maintenance. Right behind the test stand was a canal and in the evening flocks of birds would start flying in to roost for the night next to the waterway. We got the bright idea to shoot at them (PETA and birders would frown on this) with an air cannon.

A five or six foot long piece of two inch pipe was found and welded shut at one end with an Aeroquip fitting attached. The fitting was attached to a high pressure compressed air source with a ball valve controlling the on/off airflow. We stuffed a paper wad down the barrel followed by nuts, bolts, screws, ball bearings and assorted small parts.

At dusk birds were coming in for the night. We waited and waited until the right moment. The cannon was pointed in the approximate direction of the birds and the ball valve turned full on. Pow. It was like a huge shotgun going off and the birds scattered. I'm not sure if we actually got any of them, but we disconnected and hid the cannon for possible use on another evening. Grown men acting like kids. Can you believe it?

On my first days at C10 test area I observed that there was a large washed out area behind the engine. The jet blast had eroded away the vegetation and the sandy earth for perhaps one hundred feet in length, fifty feet in width and several feet in depth . In the middle of this washed out area was the remnants of a dried up live oak tree that had seen better days.

Engineers who had preceded me in this assignment all wanted to be the one who blew over the big tree with the jet engine blast. None had succeeded thus far. Now it was my turn. I got the bright idea to tie a big tarp behind the tree to assist in blowing it down.

One of the test crew men climbed up the tree to near the top and tied four hefty ropes to it and to the four corners of the tarp. The next day as we were running the engine, the tarp inflated as planned and was pulling on the tree like a parachute. The plan was working. Just then, we noticed that the test manager had come out of the office building with a bunch of customers to let them see and hear a JT9D engine being tested. They first looked at the engine and then spotted the tree with the parachute attached to it. The manager laughed, shook his head and said something to the customers. It probably was "boys will be boys." That old tree was eventually knocked down on my watch, so I had bragging rights.

After shutdown of the engine, the washed out area was dry from jet blast, but before too long it slowly filled with water again. When the engine was started, water would be blown out first followed by more erosion of the sand. After one shutdown, we noticed a small alligator about three feet long crawling in the washout.

We ran over to it and one of the crew grabbed a stick to hold its head down. I grabbed the alligator behind the head and near its rear legs and picked it up. They say that if you turn an alligator on its back it gets lethargic and almost falls asleep. I did that and, for some crazy reason, decided to go into the office to show the secretaries. They responded with screams, laughs and otherwise mixed emotions. I eventually returned the little guy to the canal behind the test stand and let him go.

One weekend I checked in at the test stand with instructions for the crew. A security supervisor was called to let me in to the test area. When I was leaving, I placed a call to the security desk to open the gate for me to leave. As I was waiting near the guard shack, I spotted two huge alligators in the adjacent pond.

To amuse myself, I picked up a few stones and started chucking them in their direction. Before long they both turned and started to slowly swim towards me. As they approached the shoreline, I started to back up to keep my distance from them. The word is that they can move really fast on land in a straight line. An evasive move would be to zig zag in different directions to avoid them but I was not going to test that theory on this particular day.

Before long I was backed up to the guard shack and both gators were out of the water with bellies off the ground in attack mode. Oh, shit, where the hell was the guard to open the gate for me? There are reasons why all of the security guards carry loaded weapons here in Florida and this is one of them.

I retreated to the main building and called security again. They said they were on their way. By the time the guard got there, the gators had disappeared. It was time to get out of there and head back to the coast.

While driving on the long road from the test area to the main assembly plant one day, I spotted an object in the road. It must have been something that fell off a truck, I thought.

As I got closer, I could see it was a big snake coiled up on the centerline of the road. I did not plan on hitting the snake, so I just stayed in my lane to pass by it. As I did so, the snake lunged at the car. Whump.

I looked in the rearview mirror and saw the snake flopping around in the road. God, I hate snakes, especially big, aggressive ones. Alligators don't bother me as much as snakes, though. You just have to be careful around them. One night I was driving back to the coast on the Bee Line and a five foot alligator slithered right in front of the car. I could not avoid hitting it, so I ran over it. They must be made of a lot of water because it just went "squish."

The Bee Line is a dangerous highway. It is only one lane in each direction and cars are traveling at least sixty mph. That's a 120 mph closing speed. Traffic gets busy at shift change. People are anxious to get home and passing is frequent. One young engineer who followed me as a volunteer for duty at the test stand died later that year as he was coming into work. Someone leaving work pulled out to pass and hit him head on. His car was catapulted into a drainage ditch at the side of the road and he died at the scene of the accident. Could have been me.

22. LEAVING FLORIDA

We were enjoying our stay in Florida. Brenda bought a bicycle with a child carrier seat on the back for our daughter, Kimberly, and they went pedaling around Singer Island. The island was fairly rural at the time with only one high rise condominium on the beach. There were some private homes, a few motels and marinas but not much else. We had been staying at Tahiti on the Ocean, but Pratt decided this place was too expensive so we had to move. The same people who owned this motel had another one nearby. It was called Tahiti on the Inlet. It was cheaper, but still nice with a pool and a view of the Palm Beach Inlet.

Boats were constantly going in and out of the inlet including huge Tropicana ships transporting oranges and grapefruit. I fished the inlet on occasion. One time I hooked a good size fish and was reeling it in, when all of a sudden a larger fish streaked by and grabbed it. I never saw what the attacking fish was, but suspect it was a barracuda or shark.

Another time when fishing the inlet, I spotted a scuba diver surfacing nearby. I wouldn't think diving in an inlet with boat traffic and strong currents was a good idea, but this diver had speared a big grouper and it was dragging him all over the inlet. He managed to get to the rocky edge of the inlet and called out to me for help. I assisted him by pulling the fish up on the rocks as he rested and recovered from his ordeal. Nice fish but was it worth the risk?

Brenda and Kimberly out for a bike ride on Singer Island, West Palm Beach, Florida, 1974.

Kimberly was going to turn two years old, so we decided to travel to Walt Disney World in Orlando to celebrate her birthday on the weekend. We stayed at the Contemporary Hotel which was fairly new at the time and unique because the monorail went right through the building. When we left WPB, it was warm and humid but when we arrived at Disney World, it was much cooler so we had to buy sweatshirts and jackets to stay warm. We learned that Florida is an interesting state in that it can sometimes have three temperature zones.

We had definitely shifted into a cooler zone.

It was a fun visit even though Kimberly was a little shy having her picture taken with the Disney characters. We celebrated Kimberly's second birthday on April 7th, 1972. On our way back to WPB, we decided to spend an extra day at Sea World. When we tried to check into a hotel for the evening, they would not accept a check and we were running low on cash. We did not have a credit card at the time and our only source of money was in our WPB checking account. Bummer. We would have to cut our vacation time short and high tail it back to WPB. It wasn't long after that that we obtained our first credit card. Lesson learned.

Kimberly (two years old) on her tricycle, West Palm Beach, Florida, 1974. One of my favorite pictures of her.

The engine endurance program was going to have some down time. Brenda was not feeling too well for whatever reason and so we made the decision to drive back to Connecticut. We left the rental car at the hotel and headed north in the Pinto. I would fly back to Florida in a couple of weeks and return to my duties as the test engineer at C10. We were to find out that Brenda was experiencing morning sickness because she was pregnant. Our second child was on the way. How exciting is that.

But in the meantime I had to return to Florida to finish the engine endurance program. I was able to get on the company Boeing 727 that was based at Rentschler Field and flew directly to the Pratt facility. It was nice flying on this airplane because it was set up for business travelers including luxury seating and a conference room. As we took off on our flight south, the airplane must have been at full capacity because I can remember the wheels were still on the ground as we passed the intersection of two runways at one end of the field. We just cleared the blast fence that was near the road at the end of the runway. That was cutting it pretty close and I breathed a sigh of relief to be safely in the air.

I was at C10 one weekend which also coincided with a rock concert being held nearby at a race car stadium just off the Bee Line Highway. After completing my duties at the test stand and giving instructions for my crew to continue on with the program, I attempted to make my way back to the coast. As I approached the highway, I could not turn east because it was blocked with thousands of people on foot trying to get to the stadium to the west. They had parked or abandoned their cars and were walking the last couple of miles to the stadium.

My only alternative was to turn west towards Indiantown and go with the flow of people. This had to have been what Woodstock, New York was like a few years ago in August of 1969.

The crowd of hippies, probably high on marihuana and booze, making their way en masse to a concert was pretty scary. I inched along with the rented Oldsmobile at the pace of the foot traffic.

The people were nice enough and in a concert mood, but I kept the windows up and the doors locked just in case. The mob was all around me and I could hear the sound of beer can pop tops scraping the side of the car. I could do nothing about it, so I just continued to drive and hope that I didn't hit anybody.

After a while I reached the stadium where the rock concert was going to be held and the crowd started to dissipate as they left the highway and headed towards the stadium entrance. I was trapped in that crowd for over an hour, but it seemed much longer than that. I was glad to leave the concertgoers behind as I headed west towards Indiantown and then east towards Stuart on the coast.

It took me three hours to get back to the motel in what ordinarily was only about a half hour commute. I inspected the rental car and, surprisingly, there was no visible damage to it. I was lucky that I would not have to pay the rental company for any damages.

I commuted to C10 on Monday morning. As I drove down the Bee Line and got closer to where the concert had taken place, I was amazed at the trail of debris and cars that littered the sides of the highway. There were hung over people sleeping in and on their vehicles.

There were cars driven into the ditches and canals on both sides of the road. There were abandoned personal items including coolers and clothing all along the roadway. It was going take some time to clean up this mess. The car towing companies were going to be real busy for quite awhile. And it did take almost a week to clear up the mess. I hope that the concertgoers had a good time after all their efforts to get to the stadium and then get out of there afterwards. Not my cup of tea to be sure. I was an old married man.

We completed the endurance program at C10 and prepared to have the engine shipped back to East Hartford. As the crew rolled some equipment out of the way to dismount the engine, they ran over a pygmy rattlesnake. Geez, I hate those snakes, or any snake for that matter.

The truck drivers who were consigned to transport the engine asked me when I wanted it back in East Hartford. I figured it would take a couple of days at least, but with two drivers they could be there in twenty-four hours by driving nonstop. I told them there was no rush. As it turns out, I flew back on the company plane and arrived before the engine got delivered. Pratt was sponsoring an air show at Rentschler Field this particular weekend and as we landed and taxied to the hanger, we were surrounded by military planes, biplanes, a Ford Trimotor, and all kinds of show aircraft. It felt like we were part of the air show as we taxied to the hanger.

When our test engine finally arrived in East Hartford, I got a call to come down to where they unloaded it from the truck. There were snakes all over the place and they wanted me to determine if they were poisonous or not. Turns out a mamma snake was hiding in the shipping buck and gave birth to a bunch of babies during transit. They were just corn snakes and not venomous. We killed them all. Have I mentioned that I still hate snakes to this day?

23. BENTLEY

It was back to reality in Connecticut after having completed two tours of duty at the Pratt plant in Florida. We had our new house in Coventry and we were settling in with our two year old daughter, Kimberly. Brenda was pregnant with our second child. Work was going well in East Hartford and I was enjoying the JT9D experimental engine test program that I was assigned to. Life was good.

I had been introduced to hunting at an early age. My dad hunted small game most of his life but pheasant hunting was his favorite. He had a couple of hunting dogs but the best one was Rex, an Irish setter.

This breed of dog is known as a pointer. As a pointer zeros in on its prey, it slowly approaches with tail straight out and nose pointed at its intended target. When you see this behavior you know a bird is going to launch into the air at any moment. Now is the time to flick the safety off on the shotgun and be prepared to shoot because you know what's coming. This is the thrill of hunting as a team with a dog.

If you did not have a dog to work with, you might walk right by the game. Dad told me that Rex got so close to a cock pheasant one time that the bird aggressively jumped up and clawed him right in the face. On their last hunting trip, Rex was getting old and had trouble just getting up from his bed in the morning. My dad picked him up and carried him to the car.

At the hunting grounds, Rex was energized enough to get his legs under him and he performed well all morning. This would be his last hunt. He died that night. The bond between human and animal is hard to explain. I'm sure my dad cried as he buried Rex in the back yard the next day. It is not an easy thing to do. I have cried more for putting an animal down than I have for some relatives.

My dad went on to get another dog, Lady Pepper, which was an English setter. This is the dog that I grew up with. She turned out to be gun shy and would run home when the first shot was fired. I guess my dad already had the one good dog you are allowed in life, and that was Rex. I was with my dad when we put Lady Pepper down. She was injected by the vet while I was holding her and she took her last breath in my arms. Is this what life and death is all about? I was devastated.

I had been hunting occasionally with mixed results. One morning I got out of the car, stepped over a stone wall, loaded my shotgun and started walking through a field. Within a few minutes I stepped on a cock pheasant and it exploded into flight with its wings literally hitting my shins as it took off. I was so rattled when I raised the gun to my shoulder that I missed an easy straight away shot at the fleeing bird. It took me awhile to settle down from the surprise shock. Man, did that get my heart beating.

If I had a dog, it would have scented that bird and given me some advance notice so I could get ready to shoot. I think that was the moment I decided to get a hunting dog. Of all the breeds out there, for some reason I decided to get a Springer spaniel. A friend who had a Springer led me to a breeder that had a litter for sale.

As I viewed the puppies at the breeder's home, there was one who stood out. The puppies, there were perhaps ten of them, sat at attention looking at their mom but one was looking in the opposite direction. I'm not sure why, but I selected the nonconforming male puppy and named him Sir Bentley of Coventry. He was a purebred and we registered him with the American Kennel Club (AKC). We would call him simply, Bentley. His mother (bitch) was named Ruby of Hickory Hill Slide, but I do not recall the sire's name.

I had Bentley in a box on the seat next to me for the trip to Coventry. He cried and whimpered all the way home. It did not take him long to assimilate into his new surroundings and become part of the family. Bentley was a happy puppy and liked to play with our daughter Kimberly. He would tug on her pant leg for some reason and Kim cried when he did that. I have a picture of a crying girl to prove it.

I worked with the puppy to respond to voice and hand signal commands which would come in handy for hunting. He loved to retrieve objects as well. It was a form of play for him. When Bentley was about three months old, we were taking a walk near lower Bolton Lake. I was tossing a stick for him to retrieve.

Kimberly and Bentley "playing" in the yard, Coventry, Connecticut, 1973.

For some reason, I decided to toss the stick into the lake and Bentley, without hesitation, jumped right in and swam to retrieve it. As he grabbed the stick and started to swim back to shore, he realized he was in over his head. He stopped swimming and let his hind feet descend to try to touch bottom. He could not touch so he swam a little closer to shore, stopped again and repeated the process until he could finally feel the sand under his rear paws. It was funny to watch, but that was the first time he ever went swimming and he loved it. I guess it is just natural instinct for a dog to swim. He was using the "doggie paddle" technique.

At the tender age of five months old, I took Bentley hunting for the first time. I didn't have high expectations, so we used this trip as a learning experience. We hunted the fields and forests of the Nathan Hale Homestead in Coventry on a spectacular Saturday morning in late October. This is one of the wildlife management areas where the state of Connecticut stocks pheasants, so I knew we would find some action sooner or later.

When a Springer spaniel gets the scent of a pheasant, their docked tail starts to wag. As the dog gets closer to its prey, the scent gets stronger and their tail starts to wag even more rapidly. Springers are flushing dogs, not pointing dogs like Setters. If you know your dog and watch their body language, it is poetry in motion and a thing of beauty. Bentley was acting "birdie" and was on to something when he suddenly flushed a nice five pound cock pheasant into the air. I flicked the safety off on my twelve gauge shotgun, put the gun to my shoulder, led the flying bird by about a foot and pulled the trigger.

One shot and down came the pheasant. Bentley was on him in a couple of seconds and was mouthing the bird. I tried to get him to retrieve the pheasant to me, but he was so excited to be on the bird that he wasn't listening to my commands. The retrieving would come with more field work, so I just congratulated him on his fine work and gave him a doggie treat. "Good boy, you got a bird."

This was the first of many pheasants, partridges and quail that I would shoot over this dog. The words "hunting" and "bird" were forever blazed into his mind and he would get extraordinarily excited every time I mentioned them. He was a hunting dog for sure and the best one I would ever have in my lifetime.

I had the occasion to go hunting with my dad one day which I had not done since I was young boy. We hunted on a farm in Willimantic that a friend of mine owned. I had stocked pheasants in the area, so I knew we would get some action sooner or later. Bentley was working the edge of the field in front of us when he finally started acting 'birdie.' I said: "Dad, he's going to flush a bird. Get ready."

Moments later, Bentley flushed a big cock pheasant and it flew to my left over a rapidly moving river. It was my shot to take. I led the bird and fired, dropping him with one shot.

I commanded Bentley to 'fetch,' so into the water he went, swimming to a small island where the bird had fallen. He picked up the pheasant in his mouth and jumped back into the raging water to retrieve it to me. Water was splashing over his head as he swam back to shore, but he made it and dropped the bird right at my feet. I never would have been able to get the bird if it had not been for this dog. Bentley was a true hunting dog and the memory of that day for my Dad and me would always be remembered. This is what hunting was all about.

I always felt that a hunting dog should be housed outside and not in the house so I made a kennel in the back yard. A chain link fence with a doghouse for shelter would be his home. Bentley was a hunting dog but he also wanted to be a family dog.

He was constantly trying to break out of "jail." One day we observed him from the kitchen window climbing up the chain link door, using his nose to uncouple the latch and swinging out into the open, riding the door as he escaped.

I should have taken this as a sign that he wanted to be closer to the family, but I was stubborn and somewhat oblivious to the needs and wants of this animal. I was determined to keep him in his kennel, so the next step was to chain him to his doghouse inside the enclosure. After that, I would find him on multiple occasions on the outside of the fence, having dug under it to escape. That was one determined dog... and I was one determined, albeit foolish, master.

I moved Bentley's doghouse to another location in our backyard. There would be no enclosure this time but only a longer chain attached to the doghouse. One chilly, drizzly night Bentley was barking in the backyard. I had finally had enough and opened a window to yell "shut up" at him.

He did stop barking and it was quiet the rest of the night. When I got up the next morning, there was Bentley laying on the ground soaking wet at the end of his chain looking at his doghouse. He had been out there all night, just laying silently in the cold. I went out to investigate what was going on.

As I approached him I said: "What's the matter, boy?" He showed me what the matter was by going into his doghouse. With a yelp, he ran back out, blood dripping from his snout and looked at me for help. I peered into the doghouse and in the corner of it was a big, mean looking muskrat. That freaking invader was the reason for the barking at night and the bite that Bentley endured trying to show me what was in his house.

I felt so bad at my failure to respond to his unusual call for help the night before. How stupid could I be to not understand the plight of my best hunting companion? I have tears in my eyes as I write this and realize that I have made mistakes during my lifetime. This is one of the glaring ones.

After dispatching the invader, I unchained Bentley, took him inside, cleaned him up and made a bed for him in the downstairs family room. There would be no more sleeping outside for my furry hunting buddy. Lessons learned.

24. LAYOFFS

B renda was pregnant with our second child. We are still convinced to this day that he was conceived under a palm tree in Florida which is pretty close to the truth. Brenda had come back from Florida experiencing morning sickness and now she was nearing full term.

I was working experimental engine programs in East Hartford and enjoying every minute of it... well, most of it. One of the downsides to this business is that it was humming along 24/7 and we had to occasionally cover weekends, second shift and third shift, otherwise known as the graveyard shift. To do this, we were assigned a week on third shift starting at midnight and ending at eight in the morning. Rumor had it that working third shift would ultimately shorten your lifespan because of the disruption to your body clock and I can believe it. I wouldn't doubt that it had a lasting effect on those who worked this shift full time. After a week of third shift, we transitioned back to normal life by working a second shift, 3:00 p.m. to 12:00 p.m., on Monday and then back to first shift on Tuesday.

It was my turn to work third shift and I was in charge of running an experimental JT9D engine at the Andrew Willgoos Laboratory altitude test chamber. These are interesting test stands in that they simulate running an engine at altitude by refrigerating the inlet air and reducing air pressure by sucking down the exhaust using a number of industrial jet engines. These are very expensive tests to run because of all the energy expended for fuel, refrigeration and the sheer number of people involved.

The test stand crew consisted of an operator, assistant operator, and many instrument monitoring and recording personnel as well as a remotely located performance engineer. A number of other facility people were also operating behind the scenes equipment. I was the lead engineer directing the program, somewhat like an orchestra conductor.

We were well into the test program by the wee hours of the morning. The test stand phone rang around 4:00 a.m.. It was Brenda. I had given her the phone number of the test stand just in case she needed me. She exclaimed: "My water has broken and I need you to take me to the hospital." Oh, no. Bad timing. I couldn't leave the test stand until the program was finished and the engine was shut down.

I told her that I would be home ASAP and "Just cross your legs or something until I get there. If you absolutely cannot wait, call an ambulance." We hurried through the rest of the program. As the engine was coming down to idle

Brett (2 years old) at an outing in Coventry, Connecticut, 1976.

Kimberly (4 years old) at an outing in Coventry, Connecticut, 1976.

and the altitude producing equipment was coming off line, the operator told me to do what I had to do and he would assume responsibility for shutting down the engine. He was a good operator and I trusted him, so off I went.

The trip from East Hartford to Coventry usually took about thirty minutes. I did it in fifteen minutes. I didn't know a Ford Pinto could go one hundred mph. Actually, it couldn't. Pedal to the metal was about eighty... downhill.

I gathered up Brenda and Kimberly and off we went to the hospital in Manchester. Thankfully, we made it with time to spare. While Brenda was in labor, I dropped off our daughter in Hartford at Brenda's parent's house and then it was back to the hospital to be with Brenda. During labor, there were some issues with the baby and a decision was made to do an emergency procedure. The surgical operation went well and Brenda gave birth to a healthy baby boy. I let my mother-in-law know that Brenda had delivered by "vasectomy." Goes to show you how sleep deprivation can twist your thinking.

I later corrected my terminology to Caesarean section or C-section. We named our newborn son Richard Brett Stoebel. Now I would have even more responsibility as the breadwinner for the family, but I was enjoying being a husband and father to my children.

In my career as an engineer at Pratt & Whitney, I was subjected to many rounds of layoffs. The first one was about to take place. These are the workings of a large company. They are in business to make money. During the up and down cycles, they are either hiring or laying off personnel.

Here I was a new father with the responsibilities of a family and a house with a mortgage. It was very stressful to learn about an impending layoff. Our engineering department was ordered to be in the office at our desks on Monday morning with no exceptions. Our group had a supervisor located in an office at the corner of our room. His secretary sat just outside his cubicle. Everyone was concentrating on this area because it would be the epicenter of the layoff. I remember the supervisor talking to the secretary and she in turn picked up her phone and placed a call. Somewhere in the office, one of the phones would start ringing. It was like the kiss of death.

That person would answer the call, hang up, get up and walk to the supervisor's office. The expression on that person's face would change, and perhaps turn red, as he or she was told that they were being laid off. How embarrassing to be subjected to this in front of the entire office staff. But that's the way layoffs were conducted back then.

One of the many people who got laid off this day was a heavy, overweight engineer by the name of Bart. Bart was a good guy, even smart, but he had the tendency to doze off at his desk from time to time which was obviously frowned upon by bosses and supervisors. After he was told that he was being laid off, he gathered up his personal belongings and made his way out of the office.

I survived the morning without being called and was thankful for that. Over the years I would be subjected to many layoffs, but survived them all.

For some reason I was always in the right place at the right time or had a good boss speaking up for me. Looking back on my career at Pratt (forty-three years), I've had some really good assignments but they were sometimes accompanied by having a lousy boss. Then there were the times when I had a shitty assignment but worked for a really good boss which made the job tolerable. And then there were the sweet times, albeit far and few between, that I had a great job AND a great boss.

After this first layoff that I had just survived, I was told by my boss that I was getting a raise. Really? I was getting a raise in the wake of a layoff? Go figure. I was obviously pleased with the raise, but mourned the loss of some of my coworkers.

A few weeks later, the group was invited to a going away party for Bart at his house in Enfield, Connecticut. Brenda and I attended the party, but it was a bittersweet celebration of sorts. During the gathering, one of my fellow engineers informed Bart that I had just gotten a raise. I could have fallen through the floor. What a mean thing to say at a time like that? I can still remember the look on Bart's face when this was divulged to him.

I can't recall who made the remark but it must have been done out of jealousy or ignorance. It was an embarrassing moment for me, but I just had to shrug it off and trudge forward. There would be other moments in my career at Pratt, both good and bad, that I would contend with. This was only the beginning.

25. STRAWBERRY LANE

One of my fellow engineers that I had gotten to know at Pratt was Larry Krizan. We had similar interests in cars and airplanes. Although he never had children because of health issues in his genes that could be passed on, he and his wife at the time enjoyed our children. Larry would be referred to as "Uncle Larry" by our children over the years.

A couple of my U-control airplanes that I flew in school yards. The starburst Chipmunk was one of my favorites.

Because of our interest in airplanes, I got back into flying control line or "U" control models like I did when I was a young kid, only this time the airplanes and engines were bigger and faster. We got together in local school yards to fly our stunt planes after work or on the weekends.

We had advanced to fancy maneuvers instead of just flying level flight in a circle. We trained ourselves to fly wingovers, loops and inverted flight (had to remind myself that up is down and down is up on the elevator). Flying model airplanes was an interesting diversion from the pressures of work. We eventually transitioned to radio-controlled airplanes and continued our friendship at work, in our homes, and on the airfields. Hot rods would become a bond between us as well, but I will save that story for another chapter.

Brenda and I lived at our Coventry home for seven years. Kimberly was now attending preschool most days. Brenda was always interested in keeping busy, but was not one to join in with the "coffee clatch" crowd in our neighborhood. One could only do so much housework before getting bored.

A neighbor who worked from home approached us one day and offered Brenda a part-time job. It would consist of some secretarial work in his home and was conveniently located in our neighborhood. Brenda was very good at shorthand and office duties. This would be a great way to supplement our income.

It wasn't long, perhaps a few days of working this part-time job, that Brenda confided in me that "Cunningham" had made inappropriate advances to her by putting some music on and asking her to dance in his home office. She immediately grabbed her belongings and escaped back to the safety of our house.

When I got home from work and found out what had happened earlier that day, I was enraged. Out of the house and down the street I went to confront the SOB. Banging on his basement office door, the asshole finally emerged. I'm not even sure if his wife was home at the time and I didn't care.

No one was going to mess with my wife or children, and if they did I would put my life on the line to protect them. I can remember yelling at him, grabbing the front of his shirt, getting in his face and then punching him in the nose. He offered no explanation and no resistance. He had no defense because he knew he was wrong. That was the end of it because if he tried anything like that again, I would probably kill him... and he knew it. I would see him from time to time driving past our house with his wife but other than staring him down, that was the last of it. Peckerhead!

Our kid's activities and our shopping were taking us frequently to the neighboring town of Manchester. At some point in time, we realized it would be a good thing to just move to Manchester. It was closer to work as well.

In our travels we spotted a four bedroom, three bath Colonial style house being built in a new neighborhood. There was a sign in front of this partially completed house that it was being foreclosed on in the coming days. The builder had gone bankrupt. These were bad times. The economy was not doing well and Pratt was having another layoff.

This would be a great place to raise our children and it would be close to good schools, shopping and work. Brenda and I had many frank and intense discussions about the pros and cons of purchasing this house. What if I got laid off?

Our Tudor Colonial house at 8 Strawberry Lane, Manchester, Connecticut , 1978.

How could we afford two houses while this one was being completed? As it turns out, we missed buying the house at auction which was purchased for $45,000 by a broker (Taylor) that lived nearby. I approached the broker after the sale and offered him $49,000.00 for the house. He wouldn't even have to lift a finger and he would stand to make $4,000. He jumped at the offer.

After financing was arranged and we took out a short-term loan, I rolled up my sleeves and began working on the house to complete it as quickly as I could. There was a long list of items to be fixed and finished in order to obtain the certificate of occupancy (CO).

Work began by adding another carrying beam and lally column in the basement. My good friend Lou Zimkiewicz and his young son Mark came over to help me lift the beam into place. I was literally finishing this house from the ground up.

When the builder went bankrupt, some of the contractors came back to the house and ripped out fixtures that they had installed to try to recoup some of their money that they would surely lose in the bankruptcy and foreclosure sale. The electrical contractor even cut all of the wires to the main circuit breaker panel and ripped the panel off the basement wall. This was the only job that I subcontracted. I hired a licensed electrician to install a new panel.

I had to do some detective work to find out where the kitchen cabinets were fabricated and where the tile came from. Both of these items were incomplete and I needed to match them in order to finish kitchen and bathrooms. Through a neighboring salesperson for this home, I was able to find the source of the needed items.

I worked for six months on this house. Every spare hour after work, on weekends, and vacation time were devoted to completing this new home for our family. Finally, all of the items were completed and the town inspector signed off on the CO. We could now move into our "8 Strawberry Lane" residence.

The Coventry house went on the market through a local real estate agent. We had to push the real estate agent to advertise more on our behalf because we felt the house was not being advertised aggressively enough. As offers started to be entertained, the real estate agent asked the question: "Do you have a black couple living next door?" My response was "yes." "Would that make a difference?" Silence.

We did, indeed, have a wonderful black couple living next door to us. The husband, Alex, was a long-distance truck driver with an unblemished safety record. The wife, Helen, was a schoolteacher in Hartford. They moved to the suburbs to find a safe place for their children to grow up. There were too many robberies and killings in the city and they wanted to get away from that. Their children were lovely and well mannered.

Their boy, Roger, expressed an interest in shooting and, with his parent's permission, I taught him how to handle a pistol and rifle safely. Roger went on to become a police officer and I was proud that I had some small role in his early years of development. The Coventry house was eventually sold and we could breathe a little easier that we were down to one house and one mortgage payment.

We called "8 Strawberry Lane" our home for twenty-seven years. It was a great house and neighborhood to raise our children. We were in the new house only a week or two when my parents from Massachusetts came to visit. They were pleased with what we had accomplished in such a short time. That euphoria came to an end one morning when my dad was sitting on the toilet in the half bath on the first floor. As he flushed the toilet, the water rose and his butt got wet. Oh no!

Something was dreadfully wrong. A new problem had been discovered, a plugged sewer pipe. A local contractor was summoned. His electronic probe determined that there was blockage in the pipe out in the street. The town water and sewer department was called to dig up the street near the end of our driveway. They discovered that when the water lines were installed in the street, the contractor's backhoe had severed the sewer line. It was a good thing the problem was in the street because if it had been on our property, we would have been liable for it. We did not have a lot of extra money just lying around. Somebody upstairs was looking out for us.

26. '37 FORD

I was working for a boss by the name of Ron. He was okay at first but developed his "favorite people" as time went on and I was not one of them. Ron was very opinionated and I'm reminded of the saying, "Opinions are like assholes... everybody's got one!" I could not please this guy no matter how hard I tried. This was one of those situations during my career where the job was tolerable but the boss was an asshole. He was starting to get to me and it was affecting my personal life even to the point of not being able to go out to eat.

I actually cried on Brenda's shoulder a couple of times, but isn't that what a spouse is there for ? This is the only time in my life that I sought professional help from my primary care physician (PCP) and a psychologist. The first shrink I went to did nothing for me and tried to convince me that my problems went way back to things that my father said to me in my youth. I quickly figured out that was bullshit. After a few visits I stopped going to him.

I then hooked up with a second psychologist in Bolton. Dr. Pet took a different approach and after only a few visits to him, I was feeling much better. He got into my head and taught me how to totally relax. I started to pull out of my depression and began coping with the pressures at work. My PCP suggested that I start a hobby that would keep me busy outside of work. I loved my family and children and spent as much time with them and their activities as I could, but I needed something else to occupy my mind.

Completed 1937 Ford with Kimberly and Brett sitting on the running board.

I always liked flying model airplanes. My buddy Larry and I had transitioned into radio control (R/C) models. It was more interesting than control line flying and I taught myself how to do it.

I built a rather large six-foot polyhedral wing glider powered by a pusher Cox 049 engine. Because I knew how to fly in circles with control line, that's the approach I took with R/C. With the engine started, I hand launched into the wind and then began a shallow turn to the left maintaining an altitude of about one hundred feet. I flew in this manner, completing full circles around me until I was confident enough to attempt a right-hand turn. Once I successfully completed my first right-hand turn, I was good to go.

Larry and I flew our airplanes quite often, usually at a farmer's field in Coventry where we had gotten permission to fly. Sometimes I brought my son Brett along because he was interested in watching us fly and hanging out with "Uncle Larry."

This spare time activity was fun and it took my mind off of the stresses at work, but there was still something missing. Larry had a 1936 Ford Cabriolet that he was building at the time and I became fascinated with old hot rods.

I had started to build a car when we lived in Coventry. I had bought a partial 1932 Ford frame from the Old Ford store in Manchester. I also found a good used Buick V6 engine that I thought would work nicely in the hot rod I was designing in my head, but that project went by the wayside when I had to devote my time to finishing our new Manchester house. I just simply did not have the time to devote to a car project and so I sold the parts I had accumulated. Remembering that my PCP recommended a hobby that would take my mind off work, I decided to dive back into a car project once again.

I found a 1937 Ford two-door slant back sedan that was being advertised in the local classified ads. It was in a barn in Colchester. I fell in love with it as soon as the barn door was opened and I viewed it for the first time. It was on a rolling chassis which meant it was sitting on four wheels but it had no engine or transmission.

All of the hard-to-find parts were there like dash,

instruments, door hinges and handles, and two grilles. 1937 was the first year that Ford mounted teardrop headlights in the fenders. Before that, headlights were mounted externally, usually on a light bar spanning between fenders. There was also a humpback version of this sedan, but those were ugly and certainly less desirable.

Many of these cars were destroyed in stock car racing but this one was a survivor. I ended up taking it home for $450.00. A friend of mine flat-bedded it to our house in Manchester. I remember Brenda saying when she saw it for the first time: "You paid money for that?" I admitted that I did, but "Just you wait and see what I can turn this car into."

I worked on the '37 Ford for over a year in my spare time. Looking back on it, I probably should have been spending more time with my children, but this was my therapy for coping with stresses at work and I needed to continue with the project. The drive train for this car came from a donor 1968 Ford station wagon that I purchased from a couple in Coventry. I drove the car to Hebron, Connecticut where a friend from work, Roger, had a farm. He helped me pull the engine, transmission, rear end and a bunch of components out of it to be transplanted into the '37 Ford. In exchange for his help, I gave him one of my favorite guns which he admired… a Marlin lever action .22 caliber rifle.

I still kick myself to this day that I traded that gun away and I tried to buy it back multiple times over the years with no luck. It was a very accurate gun. I replaced that gun with another brand new Marlin years later, but it was just not the same. Life goes on.

Over the next year I did body work on the '37 which consisted of a new trunk floor that was rotted out and some minor lower body rust. Other than that, the body was in pretty good shape. The 289 cubic inch engine and automatic transmission from the station wagon went into the chassis with some modifications to the frame. I also installed the rear end from the donor car and shortened the driveshaft.

Brenda and me posing with the 1937 Ford. Plaid jackets must have been in style!

The steering column was missing so my friend Larry said he had one that he could dig up for me, literally. It was an extra steering column from his '36 Ford project (interchangeable with '37) that he had buried in his back yard. No problem. Larry got his backhoe and dug it back up. After cleaning and painting the column, it looked like brand new and the grease in the steering box was even still good. We laughed about this over the years. It was always a good story to tell to our car buddies.

I topped off the column with a banjo steering wheel which

looked really nice. After preparation of the body, I finished the car in a light brown color using lacquer paint. I painted it right in our garage and after some wet sanding and polishing, it turned out pretty doggone nice, if I do say so myself. After applying some double plastic pin striping, the body was done.

My 1937 Ford Tudor Sedan and Larry Krizan's 1936 Cabriolet getting ready to go to a car show.

I had bought a headliner kit for the interior but was having problems installing it. A call to an acquaintance, Bob Juliano, solved that problem. Bob owned a body shop in town and was the quintessential hot rod guy. He showed up at my door with a couple of buddies and with his expertise and a heat gun, they had the headliner installed in less than an hour. I was eternally grateful to Bob for helping me in my time of need and went on to do business with him many times over the years. In fact, after I got the seats installed and upholstered with seat cover kits, it was off to Bob's upholstery shop to fabricate carpeting for the car. They did beautiful work.

The car was finally completed in just over a year and we

enjoyed going to car shows and just driving it around town. I drove it up to Massachusetts one weekend to show my folks the completed project and to give them a ride. The car drove well and it was fast. Brenda took her sister Karen for a ride in it one day and exclaimed: "The thing will leave rubber if you really get on it." Too much information.

I held onto the '37 for a few years and kept it in the basement during the winter months. It just fit between the double doors of our walkout lower level. I even purchased an original 1932 Ford 5W coupe during this time period which we would illegally drive around the neighborhood with the kids in the rear rumble seat.

We took a chance doing this because it was not registered and, even worse, we had no insurance on it. This is the car that our son, Brett, jumped out of the rumble seat in the garage, tripped and landed on his head on the concrete floor. After a trip to the hospital for a grossly inflated head, he was declared to be okay by the doctors. Thanks be to God. This reminds me of something my dear old dad used to say to me … "good thing you hit your head, otherwise you might have gotten hurt." Thanks for that, dad.

After a while, I ended up selling both vehicles. The '32 went to a couple in South Windsor and we made a little money on the deal. The '37 went to a guy in New Jersey. I had invested about $4,000.00 into it and it sold for $5,500.00, so we made a little money. I had the pleasure of building and driving it around for a couple of years. I wonder where the two cars are today? I hope they are still out there giving pleasure to new owners.

27. BMX

We supported our kids for any activities they were interested in. Keep them busy and keep them out of trouble was, and still is today, the rule as far as we were concerned. Kimberly was interested in gymnastics at an early age and went to a school in Manchester in one of the old Cheney Silk Mill buildings. She was strong and did well on the balance beam and parallel bars as I recall. She then did some figure skating at the Bolton Ice Palace and demonstrated her abilities at a number of ice shows held there.

Brett began his activities at an early age with his skateboard prowess and, of course, we provided him with the necessary helmet, knee and elbow protection. He continued with his skateboarding throughout his teenage years but played some hockey on a team in South Windsor. He played that sport well into high school and still plays on adult leagues to this day.

Both Kim and Brett had bicycles that they rode quite often. Kim had no problem with me taking off her training wheels. Off she went and she never looked back. Brett, on the other hand, was a little reluctant to shed the training apparatus. I took them off and put them back on several times. One particular day, I left Brett the necessary tools to remove the training wheels himself and gave him instructions how to do it. I received a call at work later in the afternoon from Brenda who was at home recovering from pneumonia. She said: "Brett took the training wheels off his bike by himself and he is out front on the sidewalk practicing. He will be riding without them by the time you come home." Brenda was right. He taught himself to ride a bicycle. He was four years old.

It wasn't long after that we heard a local bike shop was creating a racetrack not too far from our house at the old Nike Missile Base. It was a dirt track with hills, jumps, and turns for the emerging sport of bicycle motocross (BMX). Brett expressed a desire to try this new sport so we went there on one of the race nights and checked it out. It looked like fun. Trophies were given out to the top three winners in each age class, both boys and girls. With the seed planted, in the next few days I took the fenders and chain guard off Brett's bike and installed the obligatory license plate on the handlebars. He was assigned a novice class number which we affixed to the plate. A helmet was purchased at the local bike shop and we were ready for the races to be held at the Nike site the following week.

During the week prior to the next race, we went to the track numerous times to test it out. Kimberly also came along and rode her bike on the track just for fun. On race day, Brett was assigned a moto (race) in his novice age group. When it was his turn, he and his fellow riders lined up with their front wheels touching the starting gate. There can be up to a maximum of eight riders starting at the same time. A cadence was called out and when the gate dropped, all racers tried to get the hole shot which would put them at an advantage going into the first turn.

Brenda Stoebel of Strawberry Lane is flanked by her two dirt bike champs — Brett, 9, a 4th grader at the Keeney Street School, and Kimberly, 12, a 7th grader at Assumption Junior High School. Kimberly is ranked fourth in the U.S.

Herald photos by Pinto

Kimberly, Brett and Brenda with BMX trophies. Article from the Manchester Herald. Both kids had a partial sponsorship with Profile Racing.

Down the hill they raced and into the first berm. Peddling hard and into the second berm they went. A couple of jumps, whoop-de-doos or tabletops to clear made the racetrack interesting and tested skill level. Then, a final turn into the straightaway to the finish line and the race was over. A BMX race only lasts for about thirty to forty-five seconds, but it is fast and furious.

Kimberly and Brett with some of their BMX trophies.

Several races are run and then the top winners in each moto go on to the trophy race. Brett finished second or third that day in his class which was pretty darn good considering the equipment he was on and the experienced riders he competed against. He was enthused.

After a couple of weeks racing at the Nike Site, Kimberly expressed a desire to try this new sport of BMX, so I reluctantly stripped off her bicycle fenders, chain guard and accessories. I painted her pink bike black and purchased the required helmet and number plate.

She raced the next week and I believe there were enough girls to make up a moto (might have been combined age groups). I don't think she placed well enough to take home a trophy, but it was the start of things to come.

Over the remaining summer and fall months, both Kim and Brett raced not only at the Nike Site, but at a new track that opened up in South Windsor next to the ice rink where Brett had played hockey. Both kids started to get better and better, even with their inferior equipment. They made up for the lack of good equipment with tenacity and determination. They both did quite well, winning or placing from time to time against good competitors. They were both turned on to this sport and we would support them as long as they were willing to give it their best effort.

That winter leading up to Christmas, we started to accumulate parts for lightweight racing bikes for both Kim and Brett. If they were going to compete, they might as well have good equipment under them.

We bought the frames for their new bikes from a BMX race shop in New Jersey. After that, we were able to afford the spokes, rims, tires, cranks, gears, seats, handlebars, and all of the peripheral equipment that was necessary to outfit these specialized racing bikes.

Brenda was bringing in some pretty good 'under the counter' money from babysitting and taking in kids before and after school. That was the prime source of money to pay for the two racing bikes. Over the next few weeks I learned how to lace the hubs and rims, truing and balancing the wheels to perfection. Everything on these bikes was the lightest and latest equipment available. All up weight on these bicycles did not exceed ten pounds. The lighter they were, the faster they would accelerate. These racing bikes were presented to Kim and Brett on Christmas morning and I can still see the look on their faces when they saw them for the first time. Now they had no excuses not to be competitive.

The next spring was devoted to racing. I built a starting gate out of plywood and two-by-fours and set it up on the front sidewalk for practice. Another exercise we used to build up their legs was burnouts. Burnouts consisted of pedaling as fast as you can for as long as you can... uphill. Between practice and local racing a couple of times a week, Kim and Brett were getting pretty good.

We went to our first national race in Buffalo, New York that summer. Brett did pretty good in his motos but did not make the main event. He had a lot of competition in his age group and he had just turned from novice to expert. Now he was facing nationally ranked riders and was not the biggest kid in his age group.

Kimberly did better in her girl's class and made it to the main race. I recall that she did trophy coming in third place. Not too bad for her first national event. With a national race under their belts, Kim and Brett did better locally and the trophies started to roll in.

There were professional racers at the national events making money when they won. Amateur racers only got trophies, but at the South Windsor track you were allowed to turn in your trophy for points which could be used to purchase items in the BMX shop. Good deal.

Kim and Brett were now racing in Massachusetts, Connecticut and Rhode Island and one year both of them finished #1 in all three states. We were a proud papa and mama. Kimberly, at twelve years old, would sometimes race against the boys in her age group... and win. Her advantage was that she was maturing faster than the boys at that age and was stronger from practicing starts and burnouts. There were a lot of moms and dads, I am sure, that were not too happy that a girl was beating their boys. The next racing season would be dedicated to mostly national events.

28. NATIONAL BMX

Kimberly and Brett were competing so well in local BMX races that we collectively decided to try as many national races as possible in 1985. Kim was thirteen years old and Brett was ten at the time and they were both competing in the expert class. We upgraded their bicycles to titanium frames with a partial factory sponsorship from Profile Racing.

During a national race in Ashville, North Carolina, one of the weld joints on Brett's bike broke during practice. I quickly field stripped the bike and got a replacement frame from the Profile factory folks who were at the race with their big motor home and trailer. The new frame was assembled just in time for the first moto. I was getting pretty good at building these bikes because I had done it so many times in recent years.

One time in Nashville, a kid from Connecticut approached me and said: "Mr. Stoebel, I've got a flat tire and my race is supposed to be on the gate in five minutes." I jumped into action, replaced the tube and had him on the line with a minute to spare. The rider and his parents were impressed and very appreciative.

At that same race, I remember a little blonde girl from a nearby team struck up a conversation with us under our tent canopy. She had her younger brother with her who was cute but obviously of mixed race. During our conversation with her, she said in a southern twang: "He's almost white." I never forgot those innocent words. It came from the 'mouth of babes.'

That year (1985) we did a lot of traveling. For a weekend race, we usually took off from home base in Manchester on a Thursday night after work and drove our van and trailer all night long depending on which city we were going to. Kim and Brett would sleep at the rear of the van.

One such race was in Detroit, Michigan so our route took us up through Buffalo, New York and into Canada above Lake Erie. I usually drove the first leg of the journey until I got tired. I had worked during the day and took Friday as a vacation day. Brenda then took over and drove through the night. Give her a cup of coffee to sip on and she was good to go. I reclined in the copilot seat and got some shuteye.

At some point during the wee hours of the morning I woke up, shook the sleep from my eyes and glanced over at the instrument panel. We were zipping along at seventy mph and... we were almost out of gas. I told Brenda to take the next exit which advertised a gas station and we followed the signs off the highway to a small town. As we crept through the foggy downtown area looking for the gas station, a cop came strolling out of an alleyway. He reminded us of a London Bobby police officer with the tall helmet and night stick.

We stopped and asked where the nearest gas station was. He politely gave us directions but had to call the attendant to wake him up and get him to the station. We thanked the officer and went to find the gas station... which we never did find while wandering around in the fog. Our only alternative was to get back to the highway and try to reach Detroit on our remaining gas. Somehow, we did make it, probably running on just the fumes in the tank.

That gas station attendant back in Canada was probably still standing there wondering "where the hell are they?"

We were financing our trips to the nationals by skimming interest off of our savings accounts. Interest rates were very high as a result of the Jimmy Carter presidency whose policies screwed up the economy and would have lasting effects for years to come. It did work in our favor though for financing the costs of our national travels. I have lasting memories from all the races we attended.

We had driven out to Columbus, Ohio for a race and the weather was treacherous because of snow and ice covered roads. Exhausted from the trip, we had just checked into our hotel room when we received a call from the Caruso family who broke down about twenty-five miles from Columbus. Ronnie Caruso and her brothers were friends from Connecticut who also raced BMX. I had no alternative but to go back out into the winter conditions to retrieve them.

I was dead tired as I traveled back along the highway. Our van and trailer almost jackknifed a couple of times as I made my way back to the rest stop where they had broken down. They sure were glad to see me as we loaded all of their equipment into the trailer. Another lady, who I did not know, tried to hitch a ride to Columbus with us also, but I declined because of the liability issue.

The extra weight of people and equipment in the van actually helped our traction and we got back to the hotel safely. It probably took me two minutes to fall asleep. That weekend, both Kim and Brett qualified for their respective main races, so it was a successful trip.

During the Christmas break we decided to attend a national race in Montgomery, Alabama. With the holiday traffic, it was a long ride. It took us over thirty hours to get there, driving nonstop. Wow. The things we did for our kids. But they were very good at this BMX racing, so how could we not support them?

In Montgomery, the races were held at an indoor stadium and the racetrack was prepared by a crew from the local prison. I suppose it was good duty for them to get out into the real world and away from their jail cells. It was really warm this time of year in Alabama and we all enjoyed the mild weather. Prior to the national race, we found a local outdoor track to practice on.

Kim and Brett had fun riding there and they met some

local kids who were in awe of these nationally ranked riders and their riding skills. I'm sure they learned some things from watching our kids take the jumps with effortless abandonment. It was fun for us, too, as proud parents of our talented kids. After the races, it was back to Connecticut and the cold weather up north. Kim and Brett didn't want to leave. Brenda and I didn't either, but it was back to reality.

Pratt and Whitney had two airplanes that they were operating out of Rentschler Field, a Boeing 727 and a 737. We were able to hitch a ride to Florida on the bigger 727 to compete in a national race in Homestead. Company employees were allowed to fly on these aircraft on a space available basis. The bikes found a special location in one of the large closets on board. After the flight cleared the New York City area, Kim and Brett were invited up to the cockpit to chat with the pilots.

I knew the copilot, Hal Jensen, who had come from an engineering position in the JT9D group. He was a former military air transport pilot and was transitioning into the corporate pilot world. Unlike today with commercial airline cockpit doors closed and locked, one could walk right into the open cockpit of a private jet. It was a great experience for the kids.

After the races in Homestead, we were unable to secure seats on the company plane because it was full, so we exercised option two which was our backup flight on People's Airline. Peoples was an inexpensive, no frills airline that was operating at the time. They cut costs by collecting airfares on board the plane before it took off. There were no business class or first-class seats, only economy class.

We got the flight out of West Palm Beach to Newark. From there we would fly a connecting flight to Bradley Field. That flight was delayed. It was late Sunday night and everyone including us was getting a little punchy.

Finally, the delayed airplane arrived and, as passengers disembarked into the terminal, someone started rating them. It had to be embarrassing for the people coming off the plane. Good-looking girls would get cheers and not so good-looking people would get boos. It was funny at the time.

When our flight finally lifted off the runway, everyone erupted in applause. We finally landed in Connecticut near midnight. As I cleared the snow and ice off of our car in the long-term parking lot, I can remember spouting a few choice four letter words. Yes, it was back to reality.

After competing in national races in Michigan, Alabama, New Jersey, Pennsylvania, Florida, Massachusetts, Connecticut, Tennessee, New York, and Ohio, it was off to Louisville, Kentucky for the Grand Nationals. Kimberly and Brett had accumulated enough points to qualify for the event. It would determine their national ranking for the year.

They were already state champions in three states, but here they would be competing against the best riders in the nation. After the obligatory nonstop drive from Connecticut on Thursday night and Friday morning, we checked into our hotel. Later on Friday, we went to the track for practice.

The track was located in a beautiful park surrounded by

horse pastures. It was a very picturesque place for a Grand National race. During practice, I selected gear ratios for Kim and Brett. Gear selection was based on experience from all the tracks they competed on during the year. Finally it was time to race and staging began. I can only imagine the nerves our kids were feeling as it was finally their turn to put their front wheel against the starting gate and wait for it to drop. I know it was nerve wracking for Brenda and me standing on the side lines.

As it turned out, Brett did not qualify for the main event even though he did quite well in his motos. He accumulated enough points to be ranked number fifteen in the country which was commendable for racing in a very tough class of boys.

Kimberly did very well in her motos and qualified for the main event. As she was staging for one of her motos, a big California girl asked "Which one is Kimberly Stoebel?" She obviously had heard of Kim and knew she would eventually have to race against her.

Then came the main event. The best riders in the country were on the gate. Kimberly did not draw the best gate position, so she would have to get a good holeshot. The gate dropped and off they went down the first hill, over some jumps and into the first turn. It was a very tight race all the way around the track and into the final straightaway to the finish line. Kimberly did not have to win the race. She only had to finish in fourth place or better in points to be number one in the country. Heading to the finish line, Kim was in fourth and the California girl was in fifth. Kimberly had the advantage and held that advantage with her elbow in front of her competitor breathing down her neck. She finished the race in that very necessary fourth place spot to become the national champion in her age group. Wow. What an accomplishment and what a moment to remember.

I can still see that finish in my mind's eye to this day. To have two children compete in any sport at this level is amazing and we couldn't have been prouder of them. Hell, I have never been nationally ranked in anything in my life and probably never will. It was thrilling for all of us as a team to go through this experience together. Kim and Brett still remark to this day how it helped form who they are and how they conduct themselves in life. Hopefully, they will pass some of these lessons on to their children.

29. LIFE AFTER BMX

In 1986 we made a trip to Charlotte Motor Speedway for a spring national BMX race. Kimberly was ranked number one in her age group and Brett was number fifteen in his. They both held the number one rank in Connecticut. The National Bicycle League (NBL) had set up a track at the beginning of the final straightaway. They had brought in truck loads of clay to fashion the track from and it was expertly laid out to test all the abilities of the riders.

We did our usual walk around the course to determine which gear ratios to practice with. From those practice runs, I would get feedback that helped me to choose the final gear selection for race day. This is the way we learned to dial in track, rider and gear ratios from years of racing experience. Kim and Brett were using the standard twenty- inch wheels on their BMX bikes, but there was also a cruiser class which used larger twenty-four inch wheels. I raced that class with some of the dads and so I had an appreciation of what it feels like to race on these clay tracks.

At the start of one race that I was competing in a couple of years back, the starter called the cadence and when the gate was supposed to drop, it didn't! Most of us at the gate lurched forward in anticipation of the start, tumbling over the gate and down the starting hill. A collective moan could be heard from the crowd. We picked ourselves up, dusted ourselves off and got ready for another start. The gate dropped on the second attempt. I had witnessed this happening a number of times over the years, but this was the only time that it happened to me.

The starting line is almost always located at the top of a hill. At a track in Pennsylvania, the starting line and gate had two large flag poles on each side of the hill. Races were in progress while a storm was approaching from the west, but it was still miles away. As the riders on the gate were ready to start, a lightning bolt came out of nowhere and struck one of the flag poles.

The resulting shock was transmitted to the metal gate and jumped to the bicycles. Everyone was knocked down and people nearby sitting on fences were knocked over. After a moment, people started to pick themselves up and head for cover. Luckily, no one was seriously injured. That was a close call and, thank God, I have never seen anything like that again in my lifetime. So, my recommendation is to seek cover if you see a storm approaching because that lightning can be so unpredictable.

As the weekend of racing began, Kim and Brett were doing okay in their respective motos, but they were not racing up to what I knew was their full potential. I can't remember if they even made it to the main race at this event, but it was evident that something was wrong. Their hearts were just not in it, or so it seemed. After the weekend and in the ensuing days, we had many discussions about competing in the sport of BMX. Our budget for a year of racing was in the $10,000 range for equipment and travel expenses. If we, as a team, were not at the top of our game, then it did not make sense to continue.

Eventually, we collectively came to the conclusion that we were all burnt out from the sport and it was time to hang it up. We had met and exceeded all our goals and had memories to last us a lifetime. In the coming weeks, we started to sell off the racing equipment including our custom trailer. It was time to go on to something else.

That summer, Kimberly, Brett, Brenda's dad, Joe, and I traveled up to Riverside Park in Agawam, Massachusetts for a demolition derby. We went in our custom van with the BMX license plate on it. It was dusk when we arrived and entered the stadium. We had parked in a big parking lot and, as I was accustomed to do, I got coordinates from the alpha numeric signs on the lamp posts so I could find our vehicle when the derby was over.

Just before the show began, an announcement came over the loudspeaker that someone had left their lights on in the parking lot. The tag number that was announced was not ours, but I had a sneaky suspicion that I had left our lights on as well. I excused myself and headed back out to the lot to check on our van.

As I used the coordinates I had memorized on our way in, I could not find our vehicle. After a second coordinate check, I realized that I was looking at an empty spot where our vehicle had been parked. Our van with the custom wheels and special BMX vanity plate had been stolen! We had had a couple of vehicle break-ins in the past, but never a stolen vehicle. This was a new experience.

Let me back up a little bit. With all the miles we had traveled in this van, the engine was getting a little tired and I was starting to hear some knocking noise deep in the engine. The noise was diagnosed as main engine bearing problems. We found a mechanic that could replace the bearings from the bottom end, but it was really a temporary fix. The engine needed to be fully rebuilt or replaced. We did not have the money for that, so we opted for the temporary fix. That fix did work for a while, but slowly the bearing noise started to creep in again.

Now, if we could not recover the vehicle, it might be a blessing in disguise. I trudged back into the stadium and announced to Joe and the kids what I had discovered out in the parking lot. We needed to report the theft to security, which we did. I called Brenda to come and get us with our other car as we filled out a report at the security office. As it turned out, two vehicles had been stolen that evening, ours and a pickup truck parked nearby. It was a busy evening in the auto theft industry.

It was probably a day or two later that we got a call from the West Springfield police department that they had found our vehicle abandoned in a remote area at the end of a dead-end road. The police ordered it towed to a salvage yard and we were given the location of the yard to come and inspect it. As we pulled into the salvage yard, we spotted our custom van... it was totally destroyed. The wheels were gone, the BMX vanity plate was gone, the custom seats were gone, the CB radio was gone and anything that was not removed was destroyed. Every window was smashed and every sheet metal panel was dented or kicked in. It was a total loss. Somebody actually did us a favor and this is when the slight smile started to appear on my face. The insurance company totaled the van and we could move on to a newer vehicle, something without engine problems. This was the end of our BMX life, other than memories.

Kim and Brett had accumulated a couple of hundred trophies over the years. Some were as big as they were with clocks and telephones affixed to them. They were beautiful but they took up a lot of room and they were dust collectors. After a time, I removed all of the plaques from the trophies and kept some of the special attachments for future use. I tried to offer the trophies to various clubs that might repurpose them but this was met with little interest. I eventually scrapped the hardware and moved on. Ahhhhh, the memories!

30. VACATION & SAILPLANE

Since our kids were young, Brenda and I had been vacationing in Rhode Island. We had always felt that the Connecticut shoreline was too crowded and the water not clean enough, so we migrated to a place called Green Hill Beach. This beach was located in between Narragansett to the east and Misquamicut Beach to the west.

The place we stayed at was the Green Hill Beach Motel which was owned by a Portuguese couple and their son Anthony. The owner had built a large boulder-reinforced dune between the motel and the ocean to protect the property from storms which had almost wiped out the place during a prior hurricane. A set of wooden stairs over the dune provided access to the ocean. The beach was only lightly inhabited at any given time.

There were not too many attractions in the area. It was all about the beach. Out on Route 1, which ran along the coast, there were a few restaurants, a miniature golf course, a driving range, and a drive-in theater. We got 'fogged out' on a number of occasions while watching a movie at that old drive-in.

There was a quaint shopping area and a working farm nearby that we visited from time to time with the children. A grass airport runway and a few hangers were located between the road and the salt water pond. There was always an airplane or two to see as we passed by.

Not too far away at Watch Hill in Westerly, Rhode Island was a marina, some shops and one of the oldest and continuously operating carousels in the country, dating back to 1876. The horses were stationary and did not articulate up and down like they do on more modern carousels.

Have you ever heard of 'grabbing the brass ring?' The meaning of this is to live life to the fullest by seizing opportunities that come your way. The origins of this term come from old carousels that had a tubular tray loaded with small steel rings at the outer edge of the platform. One brass ring would be randomly loaded into the tray. As riders on the stationary outer perimeter horses passed by the tray they could grab a ring. If you were lucky enough to get the brass ring it entitled you to a free ride. Simple pleasures like this and an ice cream cone were sometimes the highlight of our day.

There were a lot of beaches along the coast similar to Green Hill, but we kept returning to this one because of its simplicity. There was Blue Shutters, East Beach, West Beach and Moonstone. A small store was within walking distance from the motel where we could purchase ice cream or candy. They also sold small fireworks and fire worms. The worms consisted of a package of small black pellets which, when lit with a match, would start to grow into a worm-like shape as they burned. Kim and Brett always asked for these. Simple entertainment. Bottle rocket fireworks were lit off after dark on the beach and were the 'big event' of our evening.

Moonstone had the reputation of being a nudist beach. We never went there, but we heard rumors about it from the locals. On one of our summer visits, Moonstone was shut down to beach traffic because a local environmental group was trying to protect the nesting grounds of the Lesser Sand Plover, a protected species of bird. Some of the Moonstone beachgoers migrated to other beaches in the area including Green Hill.

As Brenda and I were sunbathing on a blanket and our kids were occupied nearby building sand castles, a couple of young ladies strolled along the water's edge and set up blankets not too far away from us. Being a guy, I took note of this and checked on them from time to time. It wasn't long before they both had the tops of their bikinis off. I suppose this was to avoid those dreaded 'tan lines.' A little time passed and, as luck would have it, one of the young ladies reached for something in her backpack. The prevailing wind caught the object in a plastic bag and started blowing it down the beach... right at me.

Without hesitation, the topless girl got up and chased the bag until she captured it right at my side. She gave me a big smile, turned around and strolled back to her blanket without embarrassment. Whoa, wait until the guys back at the office hear about this. It will make a great story to tell over and over again.

As it turned out, Brenda was oblivious to what had just happened and the kids continued to innocently build their sand structures. All I can say is that it pays for a guy to be vigilant at a time like this. These opportunities don't come along every day. Remember, it doesn't matter where you get your appetite from, as long as you eat at home. Okay, so I admit it. I'm a pig.

My routine back home in Manchester was to read the daily paper. We actually got two newspapers. The *Hartford Courant,* which had more national news, was delivered in the morning and the *Journal Inquirer,* with more local news, was delivered in the late afternoon.

I kept seeing an advertisement for sailplane rides at Waterbury Airport. I had lots of experience with powered aircraft but had always wanted to fly a sailplane. It was on my bucket list. One day, Brenda consented and so we made an appointment for an introductory flight. Waterbury was a small airport but it was very popular for sailplane pilots because of the topography of the area and the strong updrafts off the slopes of the hills. I was introduced to the pilot in command (PIC) that would take me aloft. He was probably only about nineteen or twenty years old, but he apparently had a lot of experience and was commercially licensed to fly passengers. At the time, you could solo a sailplane at fourteen years old but had to be sixteen to solo a powered aircraft. I was now in my late thirties and it felt a little awkward having a young, snotty nosed kid take my life in his hands, but I relented.

Schweitzer sailplane.

The sailplane, or glider as it is sometimes referred to, was a two-place Schweitzer. I sat in the front seat of this tandem seat aircraft with the PIC behind me. We were towed aloft by a Cessna Bird Dog which was at one time used as a military observation plane. The hookup was made with a tow rope from the back of the Cessna to the nose on our Schweitzer. When communication between the two aircraft was given for takeoff, the Bird Dog took up the slack in the rope and applied full power.

Off we went and, because of the high aspect ratio of the Schweitzer wing, we were off the ground and into the air before the tow plane. It didn't take long to get to an altitude of about 2,000 feet. The tow plane leveled off and my PIC instructed me to grab the tow rope release knob in front of me and pull it. I did as instructed and instantly we were unhooked and on our own. The tow plane peeled off to the left and dove towards the ground for another tow job and we peeled off to the right in a well choreographed standard movement.

As soon as we released from our tow plane, we caught a thermal or up draft that lifted us another 1,000 feet to an altitude of about 3,000 feet. The sights and sounds of flying in a sailplane are wonderful. I could see a large swath of the state of Connecticut from our vantage point. There was the Long Island Sound coastline of Connecticut to the south and the city of Hartford to the east.

Noise level was just a muted rush of air which allowed verbal communication between the PIC and me. I was allowed to fly the sailplane from the front seat for about a half hour which was a thrill. When asked by the PIC, "have you ever done any aerobatics?" My answer of course was "Yes," and with my approval, the nose went down to build up airspeed and then up, up, up into a glorious wing over. How exhilarating. The 'still wet behind the ears' kid could actually fly this thing like an expert. I was impressed. But, we were getting lower now and it was time to head back to the airport for a landing.

You only get one shot at a landing in a sailplane. There is no power to 'go around' in the event of a bad approach to the runway. We were on downwind leg and I thought that we were a little high from my experience, but I was not in control of the plane. I was just along for the ride.

Turning to base leg and then final approach, we were still a little high but my PIC pulled a lever which deployed the spoilers (kind of the reverse of flaps which slow a plane, these devices on the wing would kill our lift) and down we went like an elevator. At the threshold to the grass runway and just a few feet off of the ground, the spoilers were retracted and the plane leveled out to a nice, smooth landing. Nice landing, kid. Mission accomplished. One more item checked off of my wish list. I logged the forty-five minute flight in my personal logbook as second in command in a sailplane. Nice experience.

31. TRAVEL

Kimberly and Brett were into their teenage years. Kimberly was interested in horses and, with a part time job at a local donut shop, was also saving money for her first car. Brett's interests were in skateboarding, hockey, and motorcycles. Brenda and I supported them because we felt it was important to keep them busy and let them enjoy their youth. 'Busy hands are happy hands' as the saying goes.

Now that the kids were older, Brenda was looking to earn some extra money outside the home. She had for years taken in neighborhood children before and after school and babysat on a daily basis just to earn some extra money. My job at Pratt always provided a steady income to live on but the money that Brenda contributed to the effort paid for the 'extras.' With our kids getting older, Brenda decided to branch out and get back into the workforce after a fourteen year hiatus. She started working for a dental office in Wethersfield and then moved up to a job at United Technologies Corporation which was the parent company of Pratt & Whitney.

I had never done any traveling for Pratt other than working at the test facility in West Palm Beach. I never really wanted to get into a 'travel' type of job because I didn't want to spend long periods of time away from home. Family came first for me, but I knew 'career' people at Pratt that felt the company came first and family second.

In order to advance within the company and get promoted, you had to travel. When I started in the engineering program with my Bachelor's degree under my belt, my title was engineering trainee, labor grade 42. After a short time, probably six months, I was promoted with a pay increase to junior engineer, labor grade 44.

I stayed at this level for approximately eight years until I was promoted to senior engineer, labor grade 46. It was a while before I would be considered for promotion to assistant project engineer (APE), labor grade 48. In order to get there, I had to do some traveling for the company.

One of my first travel assignments was to Northwest Orient Airlines in Minneapolis-Saint Paul, Minnesota. I went with a contingent of about six other engineers to conduct a shop visit. These visits consisted of spending a week or two with the airline's engineers reviewing shop procedures during overhaul of their Pratt engines.

We all had our areas of expertise and could make recommendations to the airline on how to better manage their overhaul practices to save money and streamline processes. It was good for the Pratt engineers also because it gave us some practical training on how our customers perceived us and how we could communicate better with them. The shop visit and trip to the Twin Cities was very interesting and productive. Northwest Orient later merged with Republic Airlines and then became part of Delta Airlines. The airline industry is constantly changing.

My next trip sometime later was to United Airlines (UAL) in San Francisco. This was another shop visit with a contingent of Pratt engineers. Collectively we worked with the airline's maintenance people to solve some problems that were plaguing their overhaul efforts. The engineers and mechanics at United appreciated our efforts and we were more than happy to share information with them. We were partners in this industry.

They had just bought some airplanes from bankrupt Pan American Airways (1991) and a lot of maintenance had to be done to get the engines (and airplanes) up to date with all of the latest service bulletins. I got to do some sightseeing while on this trip including crossing over the Golden Gate bridge and a ride on a cable car. Some UAL pilots paid a visit to our Pratt facility in Middletown soon after the shop visit and I was designated to take them on a tour.

As we stood in front of a brand new JT9D-7R4 engine on the production assembly floor, one of the pilots asked me what the engine start sequence was when they flipped switches in the cockpit. I explained to them that compressed air from the Auxiliary Power Unit (APU) is fed to the pneumatic starter on the main gearbox of the engine. As the gearbox gears begin to turn, the motion is transmitted through a lay shaft to the angle gearbox. A tower shaft from that gearbox turns a bull gear at the front of the high pressure compressor (HPC) which starts to suck air through the engine. That airflow, in turn, drives the low pressure compressor (LPC) and fan which are connected to the turbines at the rear. Once a certain RPM is obtained, ignition is turned on and then the fuel (pressurization). Once the engine is lit and starts to accelerate to idle, exhaust gas temperature (EGT) is monitored to make sure the engine is not over temperatured.

The pilots never had this explained to them before and it always amazed me that they were trained to do certain things on their checklist in the cockpit, but never knew all the intricacies of the engines they were controlling.

The next trip that I took was to Swiss Air (SWR) in Zurich, Switzerland. This was a two week shop visit to work with those folks. It was at the Zurich Airport that I got my first glimpse of military security. At every turn, there was a soldier holding an Uzi submachine gun, and they stared you down. Security was never this intense at any airport I had ever seen in the USA. As we got into the shop visit, I learned to like the SWR engineers because they drank beer at lunch. We were received very well and we accomplished our mission.

While there, we had a weekend off. Some of us took a trip to southern Germany into the black forest region. I tried to speak German with some of the locals, but they knew we were Americans and strangely didn't want to carry on a conversation in German with us. They just wanted our tourist dollars. We had lunch and a glass of wine at a castle on the Rhine River. It was beautiful with sailplanes flying overhead.

The train station in Zurich was like going back in time. It had an old world look and charm to it. Conductors directed the departure of their trains with Swiss precision. We took the train out of Zurich to Lucerne one day and had lunch next to the lake overlooking snowcapped Alpine mountains. What a beautiful city to stroll around.

At the Movenpick Hotel in Zurich, we met a young lady who offered to accompany us into town and show us some of the sights. She was very bright and, as many people in Switzerland do, she spoke the languages of all the surrounding countries. She spoke fluent English, Italian, German, and French as well as Romansh. For some reason she just took us under her wing. At the conclusion of our visit to the Swiss Air facility, we were presented with gifts from their engineers and were given lessons on how to blow the Swiss alpine horn, an instrument used by Alpine shepherds in ancient times. This was a very educational visit for me and I have lasting memories of it.

One of the longer trips that I took for Pratt was to the South African Airways (SAA) facility in Johannesburg. The trip began in New York on a British Airways flight. We were approached by a BA representative that they had room on the supersonic Concorde aircraft if we were willing to change flights. Our connecting flight out of Heathrow would not allow time to transfer, so we passed on the opportunity. As it turned out, our connecting flight was delayed and we actually could have flown the Concorde. Darn.

The delay in London allowed us time to do some sightseeing and a few of us took a double deck bus tour around Piccadilly Circus (a circular street intersection or roundabout, as we would call it in the USA). Westminster Abbey, Big Ben, and Buckingham Palace were all on the tour. It was a nice way to explore London.

With little or no sleep, we boarded our BA flight to South Africa. I loved the Boeing 747s that we were flying on because they were big and smooth... like a Cadillac. We were flying business class which gave a little more elbow and leg room. Our flight into Africa had a stopover in Nairobi, Kenya for fuel. We had a little time before departure, so I roamed around the airport shops to purchase a few items for the kids.

The armed guards there were intimidating. They did not have coordinating uniforms, they were somewhat disheveled and they didn't look like they were too well educated. They did, however, have semiautomatic weapons on them and they stared you down. Time to get back on our aircraft.

As we flew out of Nairobi, the captain apologized for the fueling delay and treated us to a flyby of Mount Kilimanjaro in Tanzania. What a beautiful sight from the air and I captured it on film. A fellow engineer, George Perzel, had a German wife who was an ardent hiker. She had hiked the entire length of the Appalachian Trail from Georgia to

Maine and was coming to Tanzania to climb Kilimanjaro. Good luck with that. Not for me.

We arrived in Johannesburg (Joberg) and checked into the Sandton Sun Hotel not too far from the SAA facility where we would be working. We had some lively discussions with local people at the bar that evening. It seems they had some disdain for us Americans, but also admired us for our freedoms, economy, and way of life. It was all in good fun.

The next morning as we were having breakfast, I noticed hundreds of black people walking along the edge of the highway near the hotel. I was told that those folks were poor blacks from the rural areas that take the train into the city and then walk to their place of employment for the day. The scene was repeated in the evening as they returned to their poor communities.

As we entered the SAA overhaul facility, we were stopped by armed guards. They asked us to get out of the rental car, we were searched for guns, contraband, bombs, and drugs and the underneath side of the car was checked with a mirror on small wheels. This was part of the daily routine that we encountered from the SAA security people. As we began working with the (exclusively white) engineers and mechanics, it became more and more apparent that blacks were excluded from the more lucrative jobs in the airline industry.

Apartheid or racial segregation existed at the time of our visit, but things would change in the near future with Nelson Mandela coming into power. The majority of people in South Africa were black, but the ruling party was made up of white Dutch and British descendants. The language was either English or Afrikaans which, oddly enough, is Germanic in origin.

The SA people were very nice to work with. I got to know one of the engineers well who liked to hunt and fish. They could not trade easily with the USA because of the segregation issue, so we struck up a deal. He gave me a list of things that he saw in a magazine from Cabela's. I would order the equipment, package it up and give it to the SAA P&W representative when he was in Connecticut. The rep would then deliver them to the engineer and he in turn wrote a check to cover the expenses. We did this transaction a couple of times and I know the SAA engineer was thrilled to have a contact from the good old USA with similar interests.

One evening our Pratt rep took us out to dinner at a small town on the outskirts of Joberg. We were taken to a restaurant in the center of a little village. There were no blacks in sight so this was obviously a 'whites only' village. The woman owner of the restaurant had a few young girls working there, one of which was her daughter—obviously a smart girl and very pretty, as I recall. She wore a button on her dress that stated 'all this and smart too.' When the owner found out we were Americans, she opened a couple bottles of wine and delivered them to our table with her compliments. They obviously liked Americans and were glad to have conversation with us. We were giving them information that they apparently longed for from 'the outside world.' Our waitress had always dreamed of going to Disney World. I hope that she was able to do that someday.

As we left the restaurant and headed back to our hotel, we encountered a large crowd of black protesters on the outskirts of the village. We would not want to break down here. We could get killed. They looked angry.

A few days later I was able to get to another town just outside of Joberg to do a little shopping. I bought some ivory gifts for Brenda and my mother and some other things for Kimberly and Brett.

Before long, our engineering entourage was ready to leave our SAA counterparts after a successful shop visit. We boarded a SAA Boeing 747 for the long flight back to England. Johannesburg Airport has a long runway, 14,000 feet to be exact. The reason for this is because it is at an altitude of 5,500 feet and airplanes need a lot of runway due to the thin air density at this altitude and hot air temperatures.

As we took off, I started to time the takeoff run. At the one minute mark, I started to get worried because the wheels were still on the ground and we had not lifted off yet. Another ten seconds later, we were finally in the air, barely. I saw the airport perimeter fence go underneath us. I could read the signs on the fence. The climb angle was very shallow as we continued to climb to cruising altitude. We must have been at max weight for this takeoff.

SAA could not fly over much of the African continent because of warring factions in the various countries, so we headed out over the western coast. If we had head winds on our route north, we were told that we may have to stop over in the Canary Islands for fuel. As it turned out, this was the longest flight that I have ever been on, thirteen hours to be exact. At around the ten hour mark, I looked out the window at the aerodynamically slim wings which contained some of the fuel tanks and wondered how could there be enough fuel stored in those wings to keep those four big Pratt engines running for this long.

There were, of course, other fuel tanks located inside the fuselage of the airplane, but I just remember looking at the wings and having that fuel supply question pop into my mind.

We did not have to stop in the Canary Islands for fuel. We landed in London without incident and transferred to a British Airways 747 for our flight back to New York. I recall the landing at JFK was pretty rough, but the pilot announced over the intercom that it was a fully automated landing which they are required to do from time to time when good weather permits. Wow, this huge airplane just landed itself. Pretty incredible technology.

32. KIDS

Time flies. Our children were now in their teenage years. Kimberly began work at a local donut shop but then went on to work at McDonald's when she was sixteen years old. I think this is where she may have developed the vegan lifestyle after having to dump containers of grease that were left over from cooking hamburgers. She was an animal lover and handling by-products of cooking meat was disgusting to her. Her goal was to earn enough money to eventually buy her first car.

After getting her driver's license, Kimberly's driving career got off to a rocky start. She was tooling around town in our family Buick with a girlfriend, pulled out in front of an oncoming car, and caused her first accident. It was all minor damage to both vehicles, but an accident nevertheless. Thank goodness nobody got hurt.

Her first car was a Mustang coupe that she purchased,

with my approval, from a private party. The car had some issues, but it was good enough to get around town. One evening, Kim and a girlfriend were driving around the Manchester Parkade where kids generally congregated. As she was passing another car in tight quarters, the driver of that car opened their door and hit the Mustang in the front fender. Instead of stopping, Kim kept going resulting in not only front fender damage, but damage down the entire side of the car.

Again, no one got hurt, which was a good thing, but you can see why insurance is so high for young people under the age of twenty-five. Fortunately, I had the body repair skills to fix the damage.

The Mustang was eventually sold and Kim bought a newer Camaro for her next car. She parked it in front of our house in a specific spot at the end of each day. One morning Kim discovered that the Camaro was not parked in the exact position she had left it the previous day. Some detective work revealed that our fourteen- year-old son, the future cop, had taken it for a joy ride with some of his friends. As the story unfolded, it was revealed that Brett almost got caught when a police patrol car pulled into a 7-11 convenience store where they had stopped for a snack. As the cop went into the store, Brett pulled out of the parking lot and high tailed it back home. Whew, that was a close one.

Our darling little boy was actually a car thief? I'm surprised I didn't kill that kid and make another one. This is the same kid that earned enough money with his paper route to secretly buy a used dirt bike without my knowledge. He kept it in the back yard covered up with a plastic tarp. And he thought I wouldn't notice it? I'm going to have to keep a closer eye on this kid in the future. Brett went on to eventually buy a bigger and better dirt bike and rode the trails behind our house.

Come to find out, those trails took Brett and his buddies to several surrounding towns. He came home with cuts and bruises from going over the handlebars on one occasion, and so it was another trip to the hospital. It wouldn't be the last trip either. I thought to myself: "If these kids survive all of the accidents, it will be a miracle."

Brett was still into hockey and he practiced taking shots in the driveway with his sister tending the net as goalie. I came home from work one evening as the sun was setting. There was a good song playing on the radio, so I paused in the driveway to listen. As I sat there listening, my eyes began scanning the gable end of our aluminum sided house.

I could see dents in the siding and the more I looked, the more I saw. There were hundreds of dents and even the vent at the peak of the roof, two stories up, was dented. You gotta be shitting me! How can someone miss the net by so much and cause so much damage with a plastic puck?

I put an end to the hockey practice in the driveway. From that moment on there would be no more slap shots using the house as a backstop. I should have been more explicit about where to practice because I came home some weeks later and noticed hundreds of dents on the sheetrock wall inside the garage. That's it, no more hockey practice at the house ever again. It took me more than a week to repair the garage wall damage. Geez, go find another sport.

I taught each of our kids to shoot handguns, rifles and shotguns. I felt it was important to instruct them in the safe handling of firearms. I learned how to shoot at an early age and I wanted my children to have the same experience. Since I always had guns in the house, I wanted my children to realize that these were not toys, but tools that, if handled correctly, were safe to be around. They gained a respect for these tools and went on to become really good shooters.

Brett was at a friend's house down the street from us when his buddy pulled his dad's loaded handgun out of the drawer for show and tell. Brett realized the danger of doing this and diffused the situation by expertly returning the gun to the drawer. He cautioned his friend against touching that gun ever again and they both avoided a bad situation because of Brett's knowledge and respect for firearms.

Brett and I got started shooting archery at a local indoor range named Hall's Arrow. It was located in the basement of a strip mall in town and catered to all ages including a program for Boy and Girl Scouts. The children of the owner were Olympic caliber archers and great role models to teach children and adults alike. Brett and I got pretty good at this game and practiced a lot.

We sometimes shot at an outdoor course in Tolland which was a challenge with stations of up to sixty yards distance. Some shots were taken between trees, others over valleys and brooks.

Brett and I qualified to shoot in the first Connecticut State games. Brett placed well in the competition and I was lucky enough to win a gold medal in the men's masters division. Eventually, we gave up on archery and I moved on to pistol competition at our local Metropolitan Shooters club. Before long, I became an officer of the club and did a stint as vice president for two years and president for another two years.

I shot in competition all over the state of Connecticut with my best scores averaging 285 out of 300. Some of the club officers pushed me into getting qualified as a National Rifle Association (NRA) pistol instructor. After obtaining my certification, we collectively taught over 1,000 students how to safely shoot and earn their concealed carry permit. I met some interesting folks along the way including a student who had been shot in a robbery in Hartford and vowed that he would not be without protection ever again.

We taught stuntmen who wanted to learn proper handling of pistols so that they did not look like amateurs in the filming of a movie. One weekend we taught a whole classroom of doctors who were reacting to the recent home invasion of a fellow professional who lost his wife and two daughters in the tragedy.

A woman judge was in one class. At the time, she could obtain a carry permit without taking any course at all, but she wanted to have the full training that we provided. Smart lady.

We taught a lot of school teachers who wanted to be trained to handle situations where students might bring a gun to school. It was very interesting being an instructor and I went on to teach for more than twenty-five years... even into retirement in Florida.

Growing up in the fairly safe town of Manchester, Connecticut was not without its dangers. Some parts of town had a migration of families from the north end of Hartford. These families came from areas where they had to be tough to survive. That mentality was brought into the school system and rivalries developed.

Brett was a strong kid and was always one to stick up for his underdog friends. This led to some confrontations with Hartford-bred gang members. On one particular evening, a trio of gang members came to our house. One of them rang the doorbell. I answered. He wanted Brett to come out and fight and I could see the other two members lurking around the corner of the house.

It would be three on one and maybe knives or guns were involved, but we would never know. As I called Brett to come to the front door and cautioned him I ran upstairs, got my Colt 45 and headed back downstairs and out the front door. When the gang members saw the gun, they clamored over each other to get back in their car and get the hell out of there. I pointed the 45 right in the drivers face and told them: "Don't you ever screw with my family again. If you do, you will end up dead."

The driver was so nervous that he stalled the car a couple of times trying to escape. That was the last time we saw these hoodlums at our house, but they did make another attempt to intercept Brett as he picked up a couple of friends for school the next morning. That family was Italian and the man of the house had a shotgun. When these guys were confronted with a .45 one day and a shotgun the next, they must have finally come to the conclusion that maybe it wasn't a good idea after all to mess with our kids. As far as I know that was the last incident involving the 'gang.'

Future incidents would occur from time to time as the kids got older. Brett must have had words with someone at a party one night because the next morning, our family Buick sedan that was sitting out in the street got the windows shot out of it.

As the story unfolded, I cautioned Brett to be careful who he confronts when he is out with friends. Words could lead to dangerous situations involving a knife or, in this case, someone with a gun. The police were notified and several .380 auto brass casings were picked up off of the street. I'm not sure if anyone was arrested in this incident, but I had some work to do to replace the shot out windows in our family sedan. So much for Manchester being 'The City of Village Charm.'

Brett bought an old Ford Bronco for his first vehicle. Of course, he had to jack it up with a lift kit so he could go off-road with it. He used my tools for this project, tools that I had owned for years from my aviation mechanic training course. Brett was new to this mechanic stuff and didn't realize that if you used a three foot long breaker bar with a 3/8" socket, the socket would break. For every tool that he broke, I made him buy a replacement. He bought a lot of replacement tools during this project but he was learning as he went along.

Brett must have pissed somebody off again because one morning when we went outside, windows were broken in his Bronco. During the night somebody had thrown rocks at the vehicle and one of them was thrown so hard that it went clear through the rear window and out the front windshield. I told Brett: "You better stop pissing people off because this is costing a lot of money to fix." Thank goodness for insurance. Kids, you gotta love them.

33. GEORGIA

Brenda was now working full time for the V2500 engineering group in Glastonbury. This program was a joint venture between Pratt & Whitney, Japanese Aero Engines Corporation and MTU Aero Engines. It was called International Aero Engines. She loved the assignment and the people she was working with and for. Brenda was happy and when mamma is happy, everyone is happy. Kim and Brett were doing well in high school and, after graduation, would either enter the workplace or continue with higher education. It was a busy time in our lives and everyone was heading in different directions, it seemed.

My job at Pratt was diversified. The nice thing about our experimental engineering program was that we got to change assignments from time to time giving us experience in the intricacies of all parts of the engine. This training would prove valuable to me in the future. Of course there were assignments from time to time that were not as exciting like QPlus (a quality initiative) and cost reduction.

The bad news is that I got assigned to cost reduction for a while. The good news is that I was working for a really good boss, so the assignment was palatable. One trip that I made was to our North Berwick, Maine facility to work with them on reducing costs.

This facility was producing compressor vanes at the time for both military and commercial engines and it was a relatively short two hour drive from central Connecticut. The Berwick folks were easy to work with and while in the area we were able to take advantage of a nice lobster dinner at the shore. I was really starting to enjoy this cost reduction assignment.

Another Pratt plant that I needed to visit on multiple occasions was our forging facility in Columbus, Georgia. To get there, I took a flight out of Bradley Airport in Windsor Locks to Atlanta, and then either fly to Columbus or rent a car to drive the one-and-a-half hours into the area. Sometimes I would go there for a solo visit and sometimes we would have an entourage of several people from various disciplines.

During one visit, I took the connecting flight into Columbus and rented a car there. The local folks appreciated the jobs that were being brought to their area by Pratt and, to show their appreciation, I was given a big Lincoln Continental rental car for the price of a cheap one. When they pulled up with the car I was shocked and, looking back on it, I should have given the attendant a much bigger tip.

The next morning I offered a ride from the hotel to the

plant to my cohorts and when they saw the car they said: "Oh, you must have contacts at the airport to get a car like this." I kept my mouth shut and just let them go on thinking that.

We were staying at a very nice hotel in the historic district of Columbus next to the Chattahoochee River. This area is steeped in Civil War history. When the Yankees fought their way into the area, all factories that were producing items to support the Confederate war machine were destroyed. Only factories producing food were spared and the converted hotel that we were staying at produced flour, so it was not destroyed.

Columbus was at the very western edge of the eastern time zone, so it was strange to have it appear so dark at the wake-up hour and so light later into the evening. I took a stroll past old homes in the historic district one evening and it was like going back in time. It must have been a beautiful place to live back in the day, and it still was to this day. There is a river walk nearby that was quite interesting where I sometimes took a morning or evening walk.

They had a vintage steam train on display that I found fascinating. One morning I climbed up into the engineer's compartment to take a look and suddenly realized that I was not alone. I spotted a couple of vagrants sleeping in the boiler compartment of the engine and I surely did not want to confront them. I slowly and quietly backed out of the cab, climbed down and got the hell out of there.

There was also a museum nearby that housed a confederate warship that plied the Chattahoochee during the Civil War. It was scuttled in 1865 towards the end of the war when the Yanks were fighting their way into the area. It laid on the bottom of the river for over a hundred years until it was discovered, raised and partially restored to its current status. I love history such as this and appreciate it even more as I get older.

People who live in the Deep South were very kind to me for the most part on my visits to the area, but there is a small part of the population that is still fighting the Civil War. They are very proud of their heritage and what they were fighting for: slavery. The Confederate flag is a symbol of that era and still flies in many areas of the south, albeit below the stars and stripes.

As I write these words, there is a move afoot to remove all vestiges of the Confederacy. The rebel flag has been demonized and statues depicting proud leaders of the movement are being torn down. As for me, I believe that southerners should keep their symbols of this past heroic effort. It is history and history should not be suppressed or rewritten. We are all Americans and should be able to express our feelings of the past. Just saying.

I developed a liking for grits at breakfast on my trips to Georgia. Of course I loaded sugar on it to make it more palatable, but it kind of grew on me after a while.

During one of my visits to the Columbus Pratt facility, some Chinese customers or subcontractors were being given a tour of the forging area. One of them was caught scooping up a small sample of a proprietory powder used in the forging process and was caught red-handed. The tour was terminated. They and their briefcases were searched before being escorted off the property and ordered not to come back. Stolen intellectual property could be analyzed and duplicated in the foreign country that they had come from.

We must be eternally vigilant. We must protect our company and our country's secrets from those who would steal from us. Research and development (R&D) costs are huge, but they are necessary for a company to develop new processes and products.

On a return trip to Connecticut, I flew from Columbus to Atlanta on a small twin turboprop commuter plane. It had a fairly sparse interior and no bath room. It probably was only a three quarter hour flight, but with taxiing, getting clearance for takeoff, etc. it could be much longer. This may be too much information (TMI) but I prepare for most flights by paying a bathroom visit just before boarding. On this particular flight everything was normal until we reached the Atlanta area.

The pilot announced to us that there was an emergency at the airport and we would be put into a holding pattern. Okay, no problem. It should be only a short time before we would be given the clearance to land. Not. We must have circled for another hour and a half before we were cleared to land. I noted that some passengers were squirming in their seats at this point. I, on the other hand, was pretty cool and collected having 'bled the lizard' before takeoff. Over the years I have encountered similar in-flight situations, like rough air, where the seatbelt sign was on and you had to stay buckled up in your seat. I file this information away under 'lessons learned.'

34. UTX

Brenda had applied for a job at the corporate headquarters of United Technologies Corporation (UTC) in Hartford and got a position working for the CFO. UTC or UTX as it was listed on the NYSE is the parent corporation of Pratt & Whitney (including International Aero Engines), Sikorsky helicopters, Hamilton Sundstrand (previously Hamilton Standard, the propeller manufacturer), Otis elevator and Carrier air conditioners. The corporate offices were on the upper floors of the twenty-six story Gold Building. There was a helicopter landing pad on the roof where executives could fly in and out of the city.

One day, there was an accident during a landing on the roof because of high winds and turbulence caused by adjacent buildings. Flight operations to the building ceased right after the landing incident. Future helicopter traffic would land and takeoff at Rentschler Field in East Hartford.

We took our kids to the Gold Building during a fourth of July celebration to watch the fireworks being fired from a barge on the Connecticut River below us. It was an interesting perspective because the exploding fireworks were rising up at us as they burst.

Brenda went on to work at the corporate office for seven years, but it became time for a change because of office politics and the complexities of dealing with corporate managers.

Brenda's next assignment was at International Aero Engines (IAE) in Glastonbury, which was a short commute from our home in Manchester. IAE was developing the new V2500 engine and Brenda worked for the VP of engineering. She loved this assignment and enjoyed going to work every day. Her boss and his wife owned a forty foot Bertram yacht that was docked at a marina in Mystic, Connecticut. All his direct reports and their spouses were invited to take a cruise with them one summer weekend. There were approximately ten couples on the boat which accommodated us well because of its size.

We were instructed where to find the life jackets and told that "Nothing goes down the toilets that you would not put in your mouth." We pushed away from the dock and headed out into Long Island sound. It was a beautiful calm day for cruising. We anchored in a Fischer's Island cove for swimming and relaxation.

After some drinks and good conversation, we weighed anchor and headed to Abbot's Seafood Restaurant in Noank where we tied up at the dock. Abbot's is known for its lobster and that is what most of us ordered. Food was served on a cafeteria style tray which you carried to your outdoor table.

We had witnessed in past visits here the aggressive nature of seagulls so we were vigilant of this problem. They attack from behind, fly over your shoulder and pick the food right off your tray. Easy pickings for them I would assume. Years later, Abbot's strung monofilament line in a grid between tall posts which discouraged the seagulls from bothering patrons. After a nice lunch, it was onto the Bertram and back to the marina to conclude our day at the shore.

Kim and Brett had both graduated from high school. Kim was attending Manchester Community College (MCC) and working at UPS. It wasn't long before she was promoted to supervisor and did a stint at Bradley Airport conducting the loading and unloading of UPS transport airplanes. Kim was, and is to this day, a smart, strong girl who could load and unload trucks faster and more precisely than the guys. I don't think the men liked her for that.

After obtaining her Associate Degree at MCC, she went on to work at Pratt & Whitney. This is where she would meet her future husband, which is a whole other story in itself. She was happy at this time in her life. Brett decided to try Central Connecticut University for his first semester of college. This was a good news, bad news chapter in his life.

The good news is that he met his future 'best man' at the school under questionable circumstances. Ivan, from Croatia, was attending the school on a basketball scholarship. He was a big boy and, luckily for Brett, he had a big heart. For some unknown reason, Brett challenged Ivan to a fight. This would not end well for Brett with Ivan saying: "Brett, you might want to think this over before you start something with me."

Ivan had lost a brother in the war in his home country and was in no mood to fight another battle here in the USA. Brett came to his senses and, as it turned out, they became best friends.

Ivan came to our house for holiday meals and felt so at home that he called us mom and dad. It turned out to be a nice relationship for all of us. The bad news is that Brett was not a good match for the liberal arts programs that were offered at Central and he only completed one year of studies there.

On an annual basis, our engine group held a conference with customers to address any problems they were having with our products. Also new innovations and service bulletins that might be in the works were presented at this forum. I had been to a couple of these conferences in the past and saw some of our presenting engineers become quite embarrassed when appearing in front of the rather large audience of airline executives. I cringed at the thought of being in that situation up on stage in front of my peers and our customers.

I was working on an experimental program with low pressure turbine modules for the JT9D group at the time. We had some problems we were working on to extend the life of the module in the field. As (bad) luck would have it, I was chosen to present information on this subject at the next conference in Los Angeles. I would be facing an audience of 700 airline experts and I was not looking forward to that.

I put together a slide presentation months in advance of the LA trip that was critiqued by fellow Pratt engineers and customer support representatives. I refined the presentation several times until it was polished enough to satisfy my superiors. We were also schooled in methods that professional public speakers use to successfully present their material. One tool was using a laser pen to point things out on the big screen. I was taught to brace my hand on the podium to steady the beam, otherwise it would probably be jumping all over the place from trembling hands. I must have gone over this presentation at least fifty times before we got to Los Angeles.

The time had arrived for us to fly out to LA. We brought our wives along and tours were provided for the girls to visit the exclusive shops on Rodeo Drive in Beverly Hills and the Queen Mary in Long Beach. It would be a fun trip for them, but not for me. Speaking in front of large groups was never my forte, but I had practiced long and hard for this conference. I was to speak on the second day of the three day event and, eventually, it was my time to go up on stage.

I was numb from the pressure of looking out over a sea of people, but I was determined to just do my best. I introduced myself and the subject I would be presenting. With laser pen in hand, held against the podium as I was trained to do, I began my half hour spiel.

I actually surprised myself, was quite professional and

got through my presentation without flubbing anything. In conclusion, I mentioned that if there were any lingering questions about anything I had presented, I could be approached in the break-out rooms later in the afternoon and we could talk one-on-one. There were no questions, thankfully, so I breathed a big sigh of relief and walked off the stage.

My boss and the vice president of the engineering program congratulated me as I came off the stage and down the stairs. I have never been so relieved to get a presentation over with. I had been working on it for months. Oh, and I hadn't eaten anything for two days prior because I didn't want to puke on stage (anxiety). Man-o-man, was I going to enjoy lunch today.

That was the last time I traveled any distance for the company and the last time I ever had to speak publicly in front of a large group. Thank goodness for that, but this conference would prepare me well for speaking in front of smaller groups in the future. Piece of cake.

35. RELATIVES

My grandparents all came from Germany in the late 1800's. My paternal grandparents were from the more industrialized northern Germany and my maternal grandparents from the southern farm and forest areas. I never got to know my dad's parents because his father had died tragically when he was only thirteen years old. I have no memory of my dad's mother. I do recall seeing a picture of me when I was a newborn with my mom's parents, though. Grandfather must have passed away by the time my grandmother came to live with us when I was five years old.

Her name was Margaret Baer and she was in a wheelchair. My parents gave up their first floor bedroom to accommodate her and I remember sitting on her lap to talk with her. I was told that she really liked that. It probably wasn't more than a year before my mother no longer could take care of her mom at our house, so my grandmother was put into a rest home in the neighboring town of Lancaster.

We went to visit her on weekends and I remember her telling my mom that she wanted to die. I did not fully understand why someone would be so desperate to say something like that, but as I go through life and witness other elderly people wishing the same thing, I began to understand that quality of life was no longer there and her wish to just end it became strong.

The only aunt and uncle that I remember on my mother's side were Arthur and Edith Baer. They lived on the same street (Chace Street) as us and about a half mile away. We visited there when I was young.

First cousins Bob and Rhonda were older than my sister and me, so we didn't spend much time together. Bob went on to become a lifer in the Marine Corps. Rhonda kept a horse in a small barn in the backyard and rode over to our house occasionally. She was an avid Elvis fan and a little bit wilder than us as I recall. We maintained a distant relationship throughout life. Both of my parents came from large families but, for whatever reason, were not really close.

I do remember one reunion on my mother's side of the family that took place at a lake side venue. Someone had drawn a family tree on a white bed sheet showing the branches and how everyone was connected. They had hired a cook to grill chicken on a large fire pit. I remember how hungry I was from swimming and playing before the meal and I can still remember the smells from the fire pit as the chicken was being basted. Sweet memories.

One of my uncles on my father's side of the family lived in Worcester. Frank and Esther lived in a three-story tenement building in the city with their only son, Frankie (Frank Junior). I remember that my sister Beverly and I did not like to go there because it was not much fun for us kids to be in the city.

Frankie was a funny guy and made us laugh, but he did not go very far in life and was still living at home with his mom and dad well into his 50's. He had served in the Army in Korea, but other than that, he never married and bounced around from trivial job to trivial job his entire life.

Frank was like a father to my dad after the death of their father. He took my dad under his wing and even bought him his first shotgun, a White Powder Wonder 16 gauge single barrel, single shot. Because dad couldn't hit anything with it, Frank sawed a couple of inches off the barrel so it would shoot a wider pattern. The gun kicked like a mule. I know, because it became my first shotgun and I still have it to this day.

Frank was in WWI and came back from the fighting in Europe with some lung disorders. He apparently was a runner between the front lines and command post. During one run, he got so thirsty and desperate for water that he took a drink from a stream that had been contaminated with mustard gas. That would affect his body later in life and so he sat in front of the TV watching baseball during our visits with failing lungs and digestive tract.

The one saving grace was that on the way home we usually stopped at an Italian grinder shop by the name of

Truro's. They made up sandwiches for us that were loaded with meat and condiments that smelled appetizingly good. We waited to eat until we got home and at the end of the half hour drive, our stomachs were growling with anticipation. The sandwiches were so stuffed with ingredients that we had to squeeze them to be able to wrap our mouths around them. Okay, that almost made the trip to Worcester worthwhile.

Dad was the youngest child in his family. He was close to Frank, but two other brothers, Bill and George, drifted apart in later years. I don't know if it was jealously or something that was said between spouses, but they were never close and I had no recollection of ever spending any quality time with them.

George and his wife actually lived in the house where my dad was brought up on Orange Street in Clinton. Somewhere in that house was an English cannon that Frank and my dad found when they were out hunting. We never did find out what happened to that historical piece.

My dad was very close to his sisters Margaret, Louise and Erna. Margaret died at an early age, but I can remember my mom saying that she admired her and was very sad at her passing. I would get to know Louise and Erna as I grew up and they became my favorites.

Louise married a Frenchman by the name of Percival Veinot. They had one daughter, my cousin Norma. Perce was a master gardener and worked for a time at an estate in Burlington, Vermont during the depression. They eventually moved back to Massachusetts and Perce began working as a gardener for several estates in the Beverly and Manchester-by-the-Sea, Massachusetts area.

One of the estates was owned by a US ambassador, so this was a prominent, exclusive area to live. Perce had a thirty-five foot lobster boat. It was a classic Maine-built boat with high bow and lap strake wood construction. He would go out to tend his traps on a daily basis and could sell most of his catch right at the dock upon his return.

Louise and Perce had a place on the little road leading to Tuck's Point where they kept the boat at a marina. A picturesque gazebo pavilion jutted out into the harbor. The house where they lived was originally the chauffeur's quarters for one of the estates and had garages on the first floor and living accommodations on the upper level.

After the Depression, the estate was being downsized and they offered the building and land to my uncle Perce at a very reasonable price. There was a large lot behind where they maintained a garden and there was a salt water inlet next to that. For whatever reason, some people in the family did not like Louise, but I really took a liking to her, and she to me. I have fond memories of this woman and a vivid recollection of her likeness in my mind to this day.

Perce was an athlete. He ran many times in the Boston marathon where my dad and mom went to watch him on several occasions. After the race, they would visit an attraction or museum in the city. On one such occasion, I remember my dad recalling the story of strolling together through one of the museums and then missing Perce. As they backtracked to look for him, they found him sitting in front of a large nude painting of a woman just studying all of the details. The women thought it was disgusting. My dad thought it was hilariously funny.

I had my first taste of lobster at the Veinot's house. On a lower terrace stood a big fire pit where Perce would light a fire in the morning. We all then went out on his lobster boat to tend the traps. Big lobster, "keepers," would go into the onboard tank and smaller ones, measured with a gauge, would be returned to the sea. After collecting the day's catch, we returned to the house with the bounty where Perce would place seaweed on the now hot rocks of the fire pit. Then lobsters, clams, and corn were placed on the bed of seaweed. Covering them up with more seaweed, they slowly steam cooked in this manner. I cannot describe how good my first lobster tasted to me, but it was so good that I went back for a second one. My parents cautioned me to slow down and not eat too fast because lobster was hard to digest. I don't know what they were talking about because I wolfed down two of them and never had a problem.

A year or two later, I was invited to spend a week at Manchester-by-the-Sea following a week at Boy Scout camp in New Hampshire. I was probably thirteen or fourteen at the time. I had gotten stung by a bee at camp and my right arm was swollen from the reaction. My parents dropped me off at Perce and Louise's and my arm slowly got better as the week progressed.

During the week Aunt Louise took me to a beach to

swim and spent some quality time with me. She made the best sweet tea I have ever tasted which was accented with a mint herb from the garden. Star fish that were collected at the beach were laid out to dry. Seagulls must have spotted them, because they disappeared from the concrete slab we had them on. There was a big, fat groundhog that resided in the back yard and it was munching on some of their garden produce.

Uncle Perce handed me a 12 gauge shotgun and a few shotgun shells and directed me to sit out in the back yard to shoot that sucker. I did as I was told and when that groundhog popped his head up out of his hole, I dropped him with one shot. Mission accomplished.

I look back on that experience and wonder if a kid could be trusted to do something like that today. Most people would think twice about handing a shotgun to a fourteen -year-old kid, but that's the way it was back in the day. Never gave it a second thought.

I went out on the lobster boat many times that week and enjoyed every minute of being with my uncle. Remember that pavilion that I mentioned earlier? He and Louise were there after church one Sunday when they heard a call from someone in distress who apparently was drowning. Without hesitation, Perce removed his wallet and watch from his pants, took off his jacket and shoes and jumped right off the pavilion railing and into the water to save that person. That's the kind of man he was. Very heroic.

I accompanied Perce to work at one of the estates under his care. The owners took pride in their property and trusted my uncle to perform caretaking duties. There was a small courtyard that was mowed once a week by Perce with a hand mower. He allowed me to mow this area one particular day. The lady owner came out and complimented me upon my completion of the yard. We had a nice conversation about my workmanship and willingness to help my uncle. Nice lady and she even gave me a tip. This concluded a wonderful week filled with memories that I cherish to this day.

Another favorite was my Aunt Erna. She was one of my dad's older sisters and the one who taught my dad to swim. How she accomplished this was a little unorthodox because she pushed him out of a boat in water over his head and said: "Sink or swim, Henry." Of course, she would rescue him if he started to drown… maybe.

She married Wallace Ackerman who worked at Grumman Aircraft on Long Island, New York as a sheet metal mechanic. They lived in Huntington Station where we would go to visit when we were kids. The first recollection I have of going there was one summer in my dad's new 1950 Pontiac.

They did not have the highways back then that they have now, so our route took us along the Berlin Turnpike where they were having gas wars. The price of gas was only twenty-five or thirty cents a gallon. I remember rival gas stations changing prices to compete for business while we were pumping gas. Then, we traveled down the Merritt Parkway and into New York. The Merritt was very scenic with ornate bridges crossing overhead every so often. The speed limit was fifty-five mph then, but they travel that road at eighty mph or more now. The new car was making a persistent clicking sound, so dad pulled over to check what was wrong. He finally realized it was the expansion joints in the concrete road causing the problem.

Aunt Erna and Uncle Wally had two girls, Audrey and Ruth, who were older than my sister Beverly and me. We got along just fine with them and their dog, Zipper. Aunt Erna was a hoot and she always made us laugh. Uncle Wally was a cool guy who took us into the basement of their house to shoot a .22 rifle into the coal bin.

He is also the guy who taught us how to play mumbly peg with a jackknife. If you have never heard of this game, it was played performing various tricks with the knife. One trick was 'over the fence' where the blade was stuck in the ground at an angle then flipped with one hand over the other simulating a fence. Another trick was simply holding the knife laying across the fingertips of a fisted hand and flipping it over until it stuck in the ground. The contest was to pass the knife from one player to another. If you were successful, you continued on to the next trick, if not, you waited until your next turn.

Dad used to call Wally the Long Island cowboy because of his driving habits. I remember he had a Studebaker at the time, and when we went for a ride with him, we held on for dear life. He accelerated, jumped on the brakes, changed lanes abruptly and drove fast. This scared the shit out of us because we were not used to navigating in New York traffic. No seatbelts either. When our summer vacation week ended and we were leaving, tears filled my eyes. I just loved these people.

Erna and Wally were always generous at Christmas time. One year as I was getting a little older, I was gifted a very nice German-made drafting set. I used this set in high school and in my first two years of college at Wentworth. I still have that set all these years later. Everyone in the Ackerman household was artistic. Wally did a painting of our house in Clinton during a visit and I still have that picture displayed to this day. When my uncle passed away, I was gifted one of his favorite rings with his initials engraved on it. Precious gift. Nice remembrances. Good people. Favorite aunt and uncle.

My sister Beverly married Walter Drohan. My parents were not thrilled about this relationship because Walter was a lot older than Beverly. As time went on, Walter was accepted into the family and he turned out to be a good match for my sister. They had one daughter, Audrey, their only child.

Walt was a funny guy and had many humorous stories to tell. I liked his sense of humor. For some crazy reason, he had one saying that stuck in my mind and it was "I'm so horny, even the crack of dawn looks good to me." I know my sister will hate me for recycling this little quip, but I just had to do it. Sorry, Sis.

Walter passed away some years ago. For some strange reason, he was not close to his two sons. At the time of his decline in health, the boys drew closer in their relationships with Walter and spent his final days together. How sad that this had to happen so late in Walter's life.

36. EDUCATION

I had earned my Bachelor of Science degree from Northrop Institute of Technology and it was serving me well in my experimental engineering job at Pratt. A little quip comes to mind because engineers, while being good with disciplines such as math and physics, are notorious for not having the best vocabulary or spelling aptitude. The saying goes 'I always wanted to be an engineer and now I are one.'

Having said that, the possibility of furthering my education with a master's degree was always on my mind, but I observed that a few fellow engineers that had an MS degree were not guaranteed to advance in the company. I was getting raises and promotions regularly without having a master's degree and I was quite comfortable with that.

Working in a large company with a variety of people and personalities was a challenge. I knew people at Pratt who were very smart who were on the fast track to managerial and VP positions, but I also knew people who stepped on toes and paid the price for it later. I prided myself on traveling the middle road and I tried to be nice to everybody which was a difficult thing to do, especially when working for an asshole boss. Just be patient, things will change I told myself.

UTC and Pratt had a wonderful education program and Brenda took advantage of it. She had secretarial school training but never obtained a degree. She always amazed me with her shorthand skills and it was useful in her early days at Pratt.

Times would change though where bosses no longer dictated to a secretary and Dictaphones came into vogue. Brenda elected to start taking courses at Manchester Community College towards an associate degree. Heck, the company was paying for it and the courses did not have to be technically oriented. The company even gave time off from work to study or attend classes. I think it was a couple of hours for each credit you were taking.

Upon graduation with an associate degree, the company awarded $5,000 in cash or UTC stock. Brenda took the stock option and paid the taxes out of pocket to reap the maximum benefit. That move paid big dividends down the road because UTC stock would split several times in the future.

Not long after obtaining her associate degree in general or business studies, Brenda decided to start taking classes working towards a bachelor's degree. She selected Bay Path University in Longmeadow, Massachusetts.

Her Saturday morning ritual was to drive to Longmeadow, grab a cup of coffee at a Dunkin Donuts drive-through and head to class. The workers at the shop got to know the routine and had coffee ready for her when she arrived at the window.

She had some great professors at this school and we have nothing but the best things to say about this University. Brenda went on to get her BA degree with a concentration in home design. Another $5,000 in UTC stock was awarded to her. You go girl!

In later years, Brenda studied at home for her master's degree from Walden University in Minneapolis, Minnesota and obtained her degree in Psychology. UTC awarded her $10,000 in stock for that degree. And, of course, she was a 4.0 student in all of her programs. I call her "my little smart-ass wife."

While she was on a roll, I urged her to go on to get her doctorate degree, but she had had enough of this intense studying while working routine. I always wanted to make a reservation at a hotel or restaurant for "Doctor and Mr. Stoebel", but it was not to be.

Kimberly took a similar path for her education, but there was a huge interruption in her (and our) lives while she was still living at home with us. Kimberly announced to us one day that she was pregnant. Oh my, what a bombshell this was.

My first thought was that she should go the abortion route and avoid all the problems associated with having a child out of wedlock. She, on the other hand, wanted to have the baby. Our first granddaughter was born and named Tuesday Paige Stoebel. Kim and Tuesday spent the next two years living at our house and a lot of the workload fell on Brenda's shoulders because Kim worked nights at UPS. As time went on, we purchased a condominium in Glastonbury for Kim and Tuesday to live in. Kim paid the monthly association fees and we paid the mortgage. During this time, Kimberly left UPS and started working for Pratt in Middletown. We still had a big role in helping to take care of our granddaughter.

Kimberly had obtained an associate degree from MCC like her mom. Now that she was working for Pratt, she enrolled in a Bachelor's program at Albertus Magnus College in New Haven. Of course, UTC would pay for the education and award her $5,000 upon completion.

Kim is a smart girl who loves math, physics and chemistry and could have been anything she wanted to be even, God forbid, an engineer like her dad. We urged her to become a veterinarian because of her love of animals, but she declined because she had the fear of having to put down an animal , which she certainly would be faced with sometime during a career as a vet. We had a cat put down one time which was traumatic for the whole family. The vet came out of the back room after doing the deed and had tears streaming down her face. She said: "It is never easy taking a life, even for a seasoned doctor."

Kimberly completed the BS program in business which was a major accomplishment while juggling work, family and school... and also a new man in her life... David.

Brett wasn't sure what he wanted to be in life, but it surely would not be an engineer. He tried a couple of semesters at Central Connecticut State University in a Sports Science program, but that was not going to work out for him. He later turned to a Criminal Justice (CJ) program at MCC and went on to graduate with an associate degree from that school just like his mom and sister.

Brett graduating from the Stamford Police Academy. Beverly, me, Walter Drohan (l-r back row). Brenda, Mom, Brett, Granddaughter Tuesday and Kimberly (l-r front row).

He was turned on by this line of study and subsequently accepted into the CJ curriculum at the University of New Haven (UNH). Forensic science professor Dr. Henry Lee was affiliated with UNH. He had testified in the O. J. Simpson trial and was known worldwide for his involvement in high profile cases. It was a great school to attend for this type of degree. Prior to graduation, Brett had been applying to various police departments to be accepted into their rookie police officer programs.

He had done an internship with the Connecticut State Police but, for some reason, did not want to go into that line of work. We suggested that he try to get into the Glastonbury police department, but that idea was quickly pooh-poohed as being too tame a town to work for. Brett wanted some excitement in his job and longed to be very pro-active as an officer.

He took the exam for the town of Stamford, Connecticut and ended up with one of the twelve positions available out of 1,200 applicants that took the test. He competed with military service vets who were given the advantage of extra points on the exam, so we know he must have tested extremely well.

After graduation from UNH, Brett entered into the boot camp rookie program at Stamford Police Academy and graduated from that. That's my boy! Many of his friends attended the graduation ceremony and it was evident that he had a cheering section in the audience when his name was called. We certainly got a kick out of that.

As I write this chapter, Kimberly is studying for her master's degree in education. Once she obtains that degree, I will be the only one in our immediate family without an MS degree. I'm feeling a little inadequate about being in that position. Will I go on to get my MS degree? Probably not at this point in my life.

37. HOT RODS

I love airplanes and still stop to stare at every plane or helicopter that flies overhead. I rebuilt and modified my own full-size Clipped Wing Piper Cub and I still fly radio-controlled planes. It's no secret that I love all things with wings, but I also love hot rod cars.

I am particularly drawn to the early Fords. The 1937 Ford that I had built earlier was a great project, but it was also a lot of work. I vowed that I would never build another one because of the intense labor that is required.

I spotted a 1930 Ford rumble seat roadster on hotrodhotline.com that caught my eye. It had been built by Jim Garcia from an original steel California car that was rust free. Jim did all of the body work on it and installed a 300 horsepower 327 cubic inch Chevy engine, 350 turbo transmission and a late 60's Jaguar independent rear end. The car was featured in *American Hotrod Magazine* and displayed at the L A Roadster show in Pomona, California.

It was purchased at this show by Richard Wickert who went on to own it for sixteen years. The car was now for sale again. After contacting Richard and receiving pictures and a build sheet, I made the decision to purchase the roadster.

It was shipped to our house in a closed trailer and I remember being like an expectant father on the day it arrived. What a sight it was to see this beautiful Porsche Red roadster come down the ramp at the back of the trailer. We would go on to take this car to many local cruise nights and we even displayed it at the Frank Maratta indoor car show in Hartford one winter. It garnered a 'best of the best' trophy and was on display right at the front entrance to the arena. How cool is that?

Having a 1930 Ford roadster was fun and I made a lot of improvements to it. The handcrafted headers had seen better days, so I removed them and updated with a set of ceramic coated headers and new exhaust pipes which I hand-fabricated. It was not much fun driving at highway speeds in this car because wind hit the flat, chopped windshield, turbulated overhead and whacked me in the back of the head. I decided to fabricate a convertible top.

I ordered a set of reproduction top irons and bows, chopped them to match the windshield height and had a local upholstery shop create the fabric top. This made the car more fun to drive at highway speeds. The rumble seat was unfinished. What fun it would be to complete this and be able to throw the grandkids in the back for a ride.

I purchased the necessary seat springs and had a local shop install the upholstery. There were no back bumpers on the car when I got it and they would be needed to allow access to the rumble seat. I purchased aftermarket bumpers and brackets and modified them to fit.

My 1930 Ford rumble seat roadster at the Villages Polo field. Picture by George Horsford for a feature in The Daily Sun.

A small round four-inch diameter step was mounted on the right side bumper and another one on top of the right side fender just like the original. Now we had access to the newly finished rumble seat. Rumble seats were phased out later on in the 1930's because they were dangerous and losing popularity. In a collision, occupants sitting in the rumble seat could be seriously injured or even decapitated. Remember, there were no seat belts or three point harnesses back then. When I take the grandkids for a ride in the rumble seat, I am very cautious where I go and it is always at low speed.

Since the roadster was a driver, I still felt the need for a project car. I had the itch to get an iconic 1932 Ford. A search online found what I thought would be a good project car. This five window (5W) coupe was being advertised by a hot rod and chassis shop in Grand Island, Nebraska. In 1932, Ford coupes came in 5W or 3W. When distinguishing between the two, the windshield was not counted. Therefore, a 5W had two door windows, two quarter windows and a rear window for a total of five windows. A 3W coupe had two door windows and a rear window only. The doors on a 3W were nicknamed suicide doors because they were hinged at the rear and opened at the front. Think Bonnie and Clyde. With this arrangement, if you opened the door while in motion, wind could rip the door out of your hand and violently whip it open resulting in bent hinges and damaged sheet metal. I wouldn't doubt that people were even ejected out of their seat if they held on to the door handle. Suicide doors went by the wayside in future years of car design for this reason.

I went ahead and purchased the 5W coupe based on photographs and many phone calls with the seller. The car was shipped from Nebraska to Connecticut on an open trailer because it was just a body shell sitting on a rolling chassis. There was not much that could be damaged from weather elements during transit.

The history of this car is interesting in that it was found abandoned in the woods by a couple of game wardens in Minnesota. The car was sold to the shop in Nebraska where they did some deceptive body work and set it on one of their aftermarket rolling (on wheels) chassis. It came with no engine or transmission, but a nine-inch Ford rear end was installed. I paid upwards of $17,000.00 for this hunk of junk including transport, but it was an original Henry Ford coupe and I was happy to get it.

There are more '32 Fords on the road now then back in 1932 because of the fiberglass and steel reproduction kits available. I wanted an original which would command more of a resale price if I ever decided to sell it.

As I inspected the car, it was evident that the body had been picked up by a forklift which bent the sheet metal at the top of the door and quarter window openings. As I got into the body work further, I found that all of the repair panels that had been welded into the bottom portion of the car were done quickly and covered over with Bondo and a coat of primer. All those panels had to be removed as well as the entire floor. This was turning into a huge project, but I was up for the task.

I ended up putting hundreds and hundreds of hours of work into this car and almost gave up on it a few times. It would be eight years before I finished, but it was a labor of love. We had a two-car garage at our 8 Strawberry Lane house which was adequate, but with a roadster, coupe and commuter cars, I really longed for a third garage that would be dedicated to my car hobby.

In the winter, I stored the roadster at a neighbor lady's house across the street. The cost was minimal and I would trade off some of it by snow blowing her driveway, sidewalk and front door walkway. Little did I know that one winter it snowed pretty much every freaking week and some of the storms dropped a couple of feet of the white stuff. The old snowblower and I got a good workout that winter.

I looked at ways of adding another garage on to our existing house, but the topography of the lot would be a challenge. It was about this time that a farm nearby had been sold to a local builder by the name of Ansaldi and he would be building a community of sixteen homes on this land.

I approached the builder because we wanted to be his first customer. As the first to commit to build, we would have the pick of the lots and we selected the prime one at the top of the hill overlooking the Connecticut River valley,, downtown Hartford, and the Metacomet Ridge seventeen miles away on the horizon.

We would use the money from the proceeds of our Strawberry Lane house and from the family inheritance. As such, we would have no mortgage on the new house and I could have my three-car garage to work in.

We selected a house plan, modified it to add a third garage and began construction in the spring. The house was located on a cul-de-sac and known as 367 Bella Vista Lane. Bella Vista translates from Italian as 'good view', and we certainly did have that. We would watch many beautiful sunsets in the coming years from our vantage point while sitting on the front steps with a glass of wine.

Since we had natural gas at this house, I had the contractor plumb a line into the third garage for a heater. The electrician installed extra receptacles in the ceiling to accommodate lots of lighting. This was going to be a great workshop for completion of the '32 coupe.

We prepared our old house on Strawberry Lane for sale. I had a local sign shop make up a metal 'For Sale' sign and mounted it on a four-by-four post that I fabricated and painted white. The sign was planted in our front yard on a Friday afternoon and by Sunday the house was sold. No real estate agent involved. The market was hot.

Our house at 367 Bella Vista Lane, Manchester, Connecticut with pillars and landscaping projects completed.

The house sold so quickly that we had to strike a deal with the new owners to allow us to rent it back until our new house was completed. Now we had to push Ansaldi to finish our new house on a timely basis because we would soon become homeless.

Since our new house was only a quarter mile walk from our old house, I went there every day to check on the progress. Of course, most days I brought a cooler filled with water, soda and beer for the workers which I think they really appreciated, especially the beer. I told them that I hoped the beer would be consumed AFTER their work was finished for the day. I didn't want them to be shitfaced while working on our new home.

We closed on 367 Bella Vista Lane in early September and not a moment too soon. Our rental agreement had come to an end, so the movers packed everything into their truck and stored it for a few days while we rented a room at one of the local hotels.

We had our niece, Nicole, living with us at the time. Nicole's mom and Brenda's younger sister, Karen, had passed away a couple of years earlier from stomach cancer. We obtained custody of Nicole and did our best to raise her the same way we raised Kimberly and Brett. It was a challenge as we would find out in time.

The '32 Ford project would be continued and finished in our new residence. I now had my third car garage workshop that was heated and washed with lots of fluorescent lighting. A work bench, MIG welder, gas welder, sixty gallon compressor, and my pneumatic tools were all at hand and I was good to go. It was a pleasure to work on my project car in this 'Man Cave.'

38. WEDDINGS & GRANDCHILDREN

Our daughter, Kimberly, was working for Pratt & Whitney at the Middletown, Connecticut plant. She had obtained her associate degree from MCC and was now going to Albertus Magnus College through the company for her bachelor's degree. She met an engineer while working there by the name of David (his last name shall be avoided to protect the guilty). This would turn out to be a good news bad news time in our lives.

David asked me for permission to marry Kimberly and I said "Yes." He seemed to be a pretty good guy at the time, but there were warning signs that we later noticed and ignored because Kimberly appeared to be happy.

Our granddaughter, Tuesday, was part of the marriage package as well. She was six years old at the time. Tuesday was a good kid and had lived with us for the first two years of her life. We spent a lot of time with her and took her to parks, museums, steam train excursions, etc. She was a 'book worm' and I tell people to this day that she read more books by the age of twelve than I have in my entire lifetime.

Wedding day was actually very nice. It took place at a Catholic church in Hebron. Because Kimberly was into horses, she wanted to be transported from the house where they were living in Hebron to the church which was about a mile away. We made arrangements to have a horse and buggy team transport my daughter and me to the church. It would be like a fairy tale wedding for Kimberly so, of course, we agreed to pay for this transportation method.

As it turns out, the horses, buggy, and two drivers were the ones that were featured in the movie *Amistad*. They were very professionally dressed in their tall hats and 18th century outfits. The horses were well groomed and embellished with bright, silver trappings. The carriage was white with gold pin striping and brass fixtures. We received a lot of looks on our way to church as people came out to the curb to wave and watch us go by.

It was a beautiful wedding day and we were very proud of our six-year-old granddaughter who read from the Bible at the podium. During the ceremony, David knelt in front of Tuesday and made a promise that he would love and care for her like his own daughter. That turned out to be a lie and none of the promises made to Kimberly and Tuesday were ever kept. Dark days, a contemptuous divorce and child custody battle would occur some ten years down the road, but that is a story for another chapter.

Not too many years later, our son Brett met a really nice Italian girl, Maria Giordano, from West Virginia. Brett had brought many nice girls home over the years but now he had graduated from college, was working for the Stamford, Connecticut police department and had his first home in Bethel. It was the time in his life where he wanted to settle down, marry a good girl, and start a family.

Brett brought Maria to our house in Manchester for the first time and we loved her from the very start. We went to a local Italian restaurant that evening and when I looked over at Maria, our eyes made contact and she broke into a big smile. I knew right there and then that she was 'the one' for Brett.

Brett proposed to Maria during a hike to one of the lighthouses on Nantucket Island. They never really made it all the way to the lighthouse because it turned out to be a further trek than they anticipated, but he did get the proposal done somewhere between the town center and Great Point. Maybe they will go back someday on an anniversary date and complete the trip.

After becoming engaged, Brett and Maria made plans for their wedding. They did not want a big church affair, so they decided to get married by a justice of the peace in a modest setting where they could also have the reception. They chose a barn that was used for occasions like this in Old Wethersfield, Connecticut. It was actually quite a nice place and my job in preparation for the wedding was to pick up some bales of hay to enhance the area around the 'altar.'

The favors to be placed on the tables were small mason jars filled with moonshine, otherwise known as white lightning, from West Virginia. To accomplish this, Maria's mom, two brothers and a sister made the trip from WV to Connecticut with about nine gallons of moonshine camouflaged somewhere in their car. They were basically smuggling liquor just like back in the day during prohibition and if they got caught they would most likely be arrested.

The trip from Clendenin, West Virginia normally took nine hours but this time it took longer because they did not want to get caught for speeding and did not want to attract attention. As luck would have it, they made the 'run' successfully. The moonshine was 150 proof, or about 75 per cent alcohol. It had a "kick" to it that would knock your socks off. The boys showed me how it burns with a blue flame.

A large tent was erected at the entrance to the barn where part of the reception was to be held. Wedding day arrived and it was raining, no, pouring. Our son was sick with emotion that they would not have the beautiful, sunny wedding day they had been hoping for. They say having rain on your wedding day is good luck. Maybe it's just an old wive's tale, but it worked for Brenda and me because it rained on our wedding day over fifty years ago and we are still together.

The ceremony was beautiful and the catered meal was delicious. It wasn't long before guests started to taste the moonshine favors at their tables. After a while, people who had never danced before in their life were on the dance floor whooping it up. Oh, the magic of white lightning!

You've seen movies where moonshine was being drunk from a jug cradled in an arm, holding the handle with couple of fingers and lifting the jug up to the mouth for a drink? Well that's what Brett, Maria and their friends did while dancing in a circle and passing the jug to one another. It was fun to watch. I think everyone got home okay that night and I'll bet they slept well, too.

That's the story of our kids getting married. Kim would go on to have three more children with 'the prince.' There was Jared, Lacey and Piper in that order. They are all different and all beautiful kids in their own way. Jared had some medical issues when he was only a few months old. He had a digestive disorder that kept him from keeping things down. He was losing weight and looked very sickly, but always had a smile on his face.

After numerous doctor appointments and even a visit to the Children's hospital in Hartford, he was getting no better. Brenda recommended that Kimberly take him to a Naturopathic doctor in Willimantic, which she did. A variety of things were recommended by this doctor including licorice. Jared responded very quickly to this treatment and soon recovered. We swear to this day that the naturopathic doctor saved Jared's life.

Brett and Maria had two children. First was Mason. Mason had us worried right from the start. We held him in our arms at the hospital when he was only a couple of hours old. His eyes were wide open and he was staring at us when any normal kid would be sleeping. Hey, it's hard work getting born. You should be sleeping, kid. Oh boy, Brett and Maria are going to have their hands full with this one.

As it turns out, Mason had very bad allergy problems right from the get go and it would take years of treatment to minimize the effects of these allergies. I'm sure there were a lot of sleepless nights centered around Mason. One night he was calling for help by saying: "Mom? Dad? Anybody??"

With all of Mason's issues, I'm surprised that Brett and Maria had another child, but the next to be born was another son, Braylon, who was totally different from his brother. I think secretly that Maria was hoping for a little girl. Would there be another child in their future? Probably not. They had their hands full with two very active and wonderful boys.

39. RETIREMENT

Our son Brett was very proactive in the Stamford Police Department. He became part of the narcotics team that did a lot of undercover work and he loved this duty. One drug bust that we found out about involved the team climbing up a fire escape stairway at the rear of a tenement building and busting down the door to enter by surprise. Brett would be the first one to enter with his AR-15 assault rifle.

As the door was being breached, shots from inside were fired through the door, one of which hit a team member in the face. This was not a good scenario and the team retreated. This was dangerous duty and luckily, the officer that was wounded went on to make a full recovery.

Of course there were light moments as well. As a result of drug busts, quite often cars were confiscated and became the property of the town. These vehicles could then be used by the task force in the performance of their duty. Some of the team members were using a beat up old car one evening when they stopped for dinner at a local Checkers restaurant.

It just so happened that this was also a cruise night with a variety of shiny muscle cars and hot rods parked in the lot. Without hesitation, the team parked amongst the show cars, got out, lifted the hood to reveal a dirty, rusted engine compartment and walked into the restaurant without saying a word. The show car guys probably didn't know what to make of this intrusion. I think it was hilarious.

Brett was involved with the narcotics team for seven years, but there was a point where this duty was starting to affect him because of the dregs of society that he had to deal with on a daily basis. To his betterment, Brett finally gave up this assignment but was still fully involved in the SWAT (special weapons and tactics) team. This team would later be referred to as SRT (special reaction team) and is the police unit that responds to high risk situations.

Brett made many fraternal friends while serving in this unit and he loved the training and discipline associated with this line of work. He would be promoted to sergeant in the future and I was given the distinct honor of pinning his badge on him at the ceremony. I couldn't be prouder of my son. He eventually went on to get his master's degree in criminal justice which he did with honors. Maybe he is setting his sights on a promotion to lieutenant? We'll just have to wait and see.

Brenda and I were now living in our new Bella Vista Lane house and I was working on my '32 Ford project on an almost daily basis. Of course, there were other projects that I completed concurrently at this house such as a stone paver patio in the back yard and stone columns at the entrance to our driveway. We were personalizing the house to our liking and I loved doing projects like this.

At work, I moved from the JT9D experimental engineering group where I had been for twenty-seven years to the PW4000 group, an up-and-coming program. We were led by an asshole program director that had taken over the JT9D and JT8D groups. He had his own agenda and personal employee favorites, so it was time to move.

The PW4000 engine was being transitioned from experimental development into the production phase and needed experienced engineers to work closely with the production folks at the Middletown plant. Barry Doucette and I were assigned to this task.

We made a good team and smoothly introduced the new engine into assembly and test at this facility. The Dick and Barry team soon built a reputation and we were recognized wherever we went. We got along with everyone. This was really great duty for two senior engineers and we were rewarded with regular raises and special awards.

I had seen a number of engines fail during test in experimental programs over the years. It was the nature of the business. But one day at Middletown test we had a production PW4000 fail. This was not good because the engine was considered to be fully developed and approved by the FAA.

While running at takeoff power, a High Pressure Turbine (HPT) disk ruptured and came out through the side of the engine. With so much energy, it almost cut the engine in two and then proceeded to cut fuel, electrical, and pneumatic lines around the concrete test cell with reckless abandon. This was a major failure that disrupted the flow of production engines going into the field and also affected engines already delivered to the customer. Production came to a halt.

The problem was diagnosed as a crack that originated in a balance flange at the rear of the second stage turbine disk. Small holes in this flange used to attach balance weights were not finished properly and were the cause of failure.

While this problem was being resolved, we continued to build engines up to the point of HPT module installation. I remember upwards of a hundred engines sitting on their fan case noses awaiting the cure. The cure came several months later and now there was a frenzy of effort to finish these engines and get them out to the field. Boeing had airplanes stacked up on the flight line waiting for engines. Such is the nature of this industry.

There were many humorous moments during my tenure in engine test facilities. One such moment came when we were testing a production engine which had to be shut down for a repair. Upon entering the test cell, we noticed a bird which had entered the inlet of the cell and became impaled on the inlet screen which protected the engine from foreign object damage (FOD).

The bird was carefully prodded off the screen with a

broom handle where it fluttered to the floor of the test cell. One of the crew members scooped it up in his hands and brought it into the control room to recover from its trauma. The engine was started and the test resumed.

It looked like the bird had recovered enough to fly again so it was gently released out the back door of the control room. The bird took flight and promptly flew directly up over the exhaust stack of the test stand where it got blown several hundred feet into the air. The last we saw of him, he was high tailing it out of the area and if he was smart he would never come back again. Stupid bird.

I spent ten years in the production assembly and test area in Middletown. Because of my extensive background, I knew these engines inside and out. I was offered a position on second shift and would be the only test engineer on duty to troubleshoot engine problems. I also had Material Review Engineer (MRE) credentials that allowed me to sign off repairs of engine parts. Although the MRE designation tended to have negative connotations, this proved to be a bonus for me and I pretty much was able to dictate my own salary. I also loved second shift for several reasons. It came with a 10% shift bonus, the thirty mile commute was during slack traffic times, and I would be able to work on my '32 Ford car project during the day.

The best reason, though, was that all of the managers went home at the end of first shift and I was able to work unhindered without meetings and all of the bullshit that happens during the day.

My only meeting was when I arrived at shift change and was briefed on important issues. I never got over the fact that the 'F' word was used fluently in these meetings with women in attendance. The 'F' word was used sometimes for emphasis in a group of guys, but I did not think it was appropriate in a mixed crowd. Times were changing I guess, but not for the better in my mind.

I worked not only on JT9D, PW4000, JT8D and V2500 commercial engines, but also on GG8 industrial engines and F100, F119 and the newest F135 military engines. The V2500 also had a military version designated the F117. Towards the end of my career I worked on the GP7200 engine which was a huge commercial engine joint venture between GE and Pratt.

I never understood the marriage of these two rival companies into this partnership, but I think it was pushed by Airbus for their huge A380 airplane. It was an awkward program and hard to manage. In any event, I had to learn the intricacies of all of these engine models and it was a challenge at times. I became known as the "go to" person at assembly and test and some managers referred to me as Dr. Stoebel. No brag, just fact. I loved my job and this was probably the best ten years of my forty-three year career at Pratt.

I was finishing my 1932 Ford project car at home and really enjoying this time in my life. Brenda went to work during the day and I had the house to myself until I went to work in the afternoon. It was a nice arrangement. Brenda was studying for her master's degree in the evening.

She was working at the UTC Research facility in East

Hartford at the time and surrounded by a bunch of doctors of science. These are strange people who were, in most cases, brilliant folks. We called them the "long haired scientists" similar to Albert Einstein. They were capable of solving complex calculations but couldn't find their own car in the parking lot. Funny, but true.

In September of 2008, Pratt announced an early retirement program for their engineering staff. Brenda heard about it during the day and mused that she would probably be hearing from me in the afternoon when I got to work and learned of it. We had been talking about retirement for some time and had actually paid a visit to The Villages in Florida in 2003 on their Lifestyles program to check out that retirement community.

We loved the idea of retiring in Florida but we were not quite ready to 'pull the trigger' at that time. We would have to be patient and wait a few more years. But, the retirement package was too much for me to resist. It entitled me to almost full pay and health insurance for a year because of my forty-three years of service.

They even asked me to work until the end of the year to help meet the engine delivery schedule where most people had to separate by the end of the month. Perfect. I was sixty-four years old and the added bonus of pay and insurance would get me to age sixty-five when I could qualify for Medicare. I took the retirement package. I would have been a fool not to.

On January 3rd, 2009, I had just finished snow blowing,

sanding, and salting the driveway for Brenda to go to work. When she came out to leave, I told her that I had to get the newspaper that was down in the street. The delivery person could not come up the driveway earlier because I had not yet cleared it of snow and ice.

Knowing the inclined driveway was still slippery, I decided to be smart and walk down to the cul-de-sac on the snow covered front lawn which would improve my footing. On the way to the lawn, I stepped on the cleared walkway to our front door, my feet went out from under me and I landed flat on my back. Black ice!

Man, did that hurt but I was helped to my feet by Brenda and I continued down to the street to get the newspaper. Brenda went off to work and I tinkered on my car project until it was time to head to Middletown in the afternoon. Even though I was officially retired, I set aside this day to clean out my office desk, say goodbye to all of the assembly and test personal, sign some paperwork and turn in my badge (S058296).

I have to admit that I had a few tears in my eyes because I had spent a lifetime working for this company and this would be the start of a new chapter. It didn't take long for me to embrace retirement. I began to smile a lot and realized all the pressure that I endured at work had suddenly been lifted off my shoulders. I tell everyone to this day that it took me a half hour to transition into retirement.

That evening when I got home, I got a big hug and a kiss from Brenda. She knew the emotional journey that I had just been through and she was there for me. After a couple of congratulatory drinks, I slipped into bed for a good night sleep and put the pain in my back from the fall earlier in the day out of my mind.

The next morning, I slipped out of bed for my obligatory whiz, got halfway to the bathroom and fell to my knees in excruciating pain. I heard a "pop" in my back which could not be good. Did I do more damage to my back in yesterday's fall than I had initially thought or was it just a muscle spasm?

Brenda reluctantly went off to work and I just relaxed to give my back a rest. As the day went on, the pain got worse. I called my honey at work and she wanted to call an ambulance. No way. All I needed was some muscle relaxant medication from our doctor and I would be fine.

Brenda advised me that the doctor would not prescribe medication without seeing me first. We made the appointment for that afternoon, but I was in so much pain I could not get into the car. Brenda drove me to the doctor's office in my truck. At least with the truck I could grab onto the A-pillar handle, step on the exterior bar and ease myself the passenger seat.

We made it to the office, my shirt came off and the doctor pointed out the spasms in my back to Brenda. I had broken at least three ribs and it would do no good to go to the ER. They would just tell me the same thing. I had broken ribs on my first day of retirement.

It was the beginning of a six week healing process. I spent a lot of time resting and sleeping in my easy chair. No grandkids or company allowed. If I caught a cold and had to cough, it would be the painful death of me. This is how I spent the first weeks of retirement. Go figure.

40. 1932 FORD

Now that I was retired, my '32 Ford car project would move along even faster. I worked on it most days now in my new heated and well lit third car garage. Bodywork was very time consuming. I had to remove old, shoddily done patch panels and redo them correctly. In some cases, there were no aftermarket patch panels to be had, so I fabricated them from scratch.

A warp in the passenger door panel could not be worked out, so I hand-fabricated a new panel by forming the compound curves using a soft-faced mallet and a boat cushion on the garage floor. I didn't have a lot of high tech equipment like an English wheel to accomplish this, so I had to improvise. I formed the transmission tunnel by bending a piece of sheet metal around the telephone pole in front of our house. Hey, whatever it takes to get the job done.

What I like about the car hobby is that there are a lot of

ways to finish one of these cars and personalize it to your own liking. I had decided from the beginning to complete this car as a "highboy" having no fenders and sitting on top of the frame. Other options could have been a "lowboy" where the body is channeled over the frame. I never contemplated building a full fender version because I wanted the 'open wheel' effect.

I told people who were not familiar with these old cars that they came in two types, standard and deluxe. The standard type was a lower cost model that came without fenders. And, they believed it.

An unchopped "highboy" '32 Ford just does not look proportionately correct to me. It looks like a telephone booth with its tall roof and no fenders. I made the decision to chop the top to lower it. This was a favorite modification for race car drivers who wanted to lower their cars to make them more aerodynamic. A mild chop could be as little as one inch, whereas a radical chop could be as much as five inches or more.

I decided on a four-inch chop in the front tapered to three and one half inches in the rear. This added complexity to lowering the lid, but my research led me to this conclusion. Brenda did not want me to chop the car, but I had made up my mind. She also said she would not ride in the car if I painted flames on it. I put flames on it anyhow and she did end up riding in it after all was said and done. Hey, this was a real hot rod and what is a hot rod without flames?

After carefully marking my cut lines, I stood there with

a die grinder and a hacksaw ready to go to work. This was my first attempt at chopping a car and, as it turned out, probably my last. Once the first cuts were made, there was no turning back. The trademark of a good chop is one where there is no evidence of the many cuts and welds necessary to accomplish this modification and I was determined to make mine flawless.

There are two ways to chop a '32 Ford.

One is to cut the roof off at the pillars, section it, move the front half forward and the rear half aft and fill in the one inch gap between the two.

The method that I chose was to cut the roof off and lay the 'A' pillars back five degrees. 'A' pillars are located on either side of the windshield. 'B' pillars are located just behind the doors which, essentially, are part of the door jam. The challenge then is to cut the windshield frame, doors and garnish moldings to match.

Many, many hours later I had completed my first chop. One of the next challenges was to repair the rusted drip moldings that channeled water away from the door openings. Some builders just remove them but I wanted all of these details to be as original. I approached a restoration shop in town to see if they could reproduce the bead portion of the drip rails for me, but they could not. So, again, innovation took over.

I ended up making my own dies and welded them to a pair of vise grips. Inch by inch I formed the bead along the entire length of drip rail by hand. This was duplicated on both sides of the car. The drip rails were then spot welded on to the roof edge and "wallah" I was done with that task.

Even though the 1932 Ford was a big improvement over the Model A (1928–1931), there was still some wood in the structure of the car body. I purchased reproduction oak wood pieces from a supplier and chopped them to match the 'B' pillars and window openings. There is also wood required above the windshield and around the roof opening. Ford was still a little behind Chevrolet in their manufacturing techniques. Chevy was now stamping the entire roof panel of their cars out of one piece of sheet metal.

Ford still relied on a two piece roof with a large opening like a sunroof. The large opening was surrounded by wood with several bows spanning the gap. Chicken wire was then stapled to the wood followed by cotton batting and waterproof fabric. After the fabric was in place, a special channel was nailed to the perimeter and filled with a rubber seal.

I found the aluminum channel at a restoration shop in Massachusetts. The problem was bending it to match the radii at the corners of the roof opening. This problem was solved by making my own wooden dies, heating the aluminum to just the right temperature to anneal it and forming it with the dies. Too high a temperature and the aluminum would just fall apart (called hot shortness), too low and it was not soft enough to bend. It took many tries and a lot of wasted material to perfect this process. I eventually won out.

I got the body in primer and selected a glossy black PPG paint color for the finish. I painted the frame, firewall, instrument panel, tank and belly of the body in my garage. A veteran professional PPG master painter friend of mine, Glenn Sinon and his dad, handled the final body prep and finishing touches for me. I built up the chassis and installed engine, transmission, brake lines, suspension, exhaust system, tank, and all the necessary components.

My 1932 Ford 5W Coupe. Picture by Bill Mitchell for a feature in The Daily Sun.

Basically, the car got built, disassembled and then reassembled after all of the paint and powder coating had been completed. This is a huge job but it is also a labor of love. UPS and FedEx trucks were delivering parts to me almost on a daily basis. It was like getting Christmas packages every day.

Once the chassis was completed and it was time to install the body, I contacted a bunch of my friends from the Connecticut Street Rod Association to help. A dozen or so guys showed up for the install with a promise of coffee and doughnuts. It didn't take long to get the body installed with this group of guys and it fit perfectly. Next up was wiring and glass. I ordered a wiring harness and switches from a national distributor. I took me three months to wire the car. I wanted the wiring to be perfect because it would be very hard to find or correct any electrical problems after the car was finished. I was able to fire up the car at this time and took my first test ride around the neighborhood without any doors installed yet. I just had to do it.

Another good friend of mine, Doug Metheny, hooked me up with a repair shop guy that could verify VIN numbers and sign off the car for registry purposes. The DMV never saw the car and it's a good thing that they didn't. They never would have given me registration papers for a car without fenders. Good friend, Brian Snell, loaded the car in his closed trailer and drove it to Willimantic for the repair shop to verify VIN.

After driving the car to East Windsor for glass installation (the windshield was already done), it was back to Glenn's garage for the flames. We had Charlie Decker, the one armed bandit, pinstripe the edges of the flames with blue paint and create a custom design on the trunk lid. His work is sheer perfection.

The car was driven to another friend, Ken Nadeau, who upholstered the interior with American Beauty Red tuck and roll leather and carpeting. Another talented guy. I cut the aluminum subpanels to attach the upholstery and worked right alongside Ken until the project was completed, saving some money along the way. Now I was ready to take the '32 to some local cruise nights and show it off.

I contacted Brian Brennen, the editor of *Street Rodder Magazine* to see if he would be willing to do a feature article on the car. I sent him some pictures. He must have liked them because he put me in touch with one of his senior writers and photo specialists, Chuck Vranas, to 'shoot' the car.

The digital photos were taken near some abandoned buildings at the old Nike Missile Base nearby. It was the perfect backdrop for an old car. The photos and article appeared in the March 2011 edition of *Street Rodder* and I couldn't have been prouder.

Having a car featured in the magazine was like hitting the lottery. This was an eight-year project that I almost gave up on a few times but I was glad that I persevered and completed the car. I now had a real hot rod that I built by myself with the help of some good friends.

I decided to take the car to some national shows while it was still new and fresh. My son loaned me his Ford F250 diesel pickup truck and I purchased a new enclosed trailer that I found advertised online. It was delivered to our house from Indiana. I prepared Brett's truck with an electric brake setup and had the local Ford dealer inspect the truck to repair anything that it needed, especially brakes. I would be hauling precious cargo behind me and I didn't want anything to go wrong.

My first trip was to the Street Rod Nationals in York, Pennsylvania during the summer of 2011. It was a good trip and the car garnered a Safety 21 award when it was reviewed by the National Street Rod Association (NSRA) inspection team. I was happy with that award because it meant the car was built well and safe to drive.

The next trip was to the Meguiar's Nationals in Syracuse, New York. Although we had a little rain from time to time, it was a nice weekend but I did not get any awards. I was invited to show the car in the Winfield Award arena, but for some reason I declined. This is a big show with nearly 8,000 cars and trucks being displayed and it is very intimidating. Many of the cars are professionally built and I did not want to try to compete with them. Over 90,000 spectators come to this event. It's huge!

The third event I went to that summer was the Goodguy's Nationals in Poughkeepsie, New York. I got some recognition at this show and the car was featured in their monthly magazine. Car shows are fun but I find that after having attended three nationals and a bunch of local cruise nights, I got burnt out. Fun for me was just driving the car locally from time to time and enjoying the adoration of spectators.

One of our big local shows in Manchester, Connecticut was the Cruising Main Street show usually held on the first Sunday in August. This year I got to drive my new '32 Ford to the show and my wife Brenda drove our 1930 Ford roadster. The show typically gets almost 1,000 cars attending and the entire downtown main street is closed off just for the show cars.

For several years we invited a bunch of friends back to our house for a beer and barbeque party. We hired a hot rod friend and fellow engineer, Bruce Baldyga and his bluegrass band, to entertain us. The weather was beautiful, we conducted tours of our new house and the driveway and cul-de-sac was filled with hot rods . I was in hot rod heaven. We hosted this party several times until one year it rained and they did not call off the show. Attendance was very poor at the show and at our party for that reason. We had leftover cases of beer that lasted us for a year after that. Did you know that beer doesn't really go bad? I can tell you from experience that it does not.

My final big show with the coupe was the Frank Marotta Show in February of 2012. I had a friend transport the car to the Expo Center in his enclosed trailer. I had sold my trailer by this time and actually got more money for it than what I had paid initially. What a deal.

I was given a prime spot at the show and really enjoyed all the attention that the car got. I was awarded a 'Best of the Best' trophy which I still proudly display to this day in my garage 'Man Cave.'

Some of my friends built Chevy's and some enjoyed muscle cars, trucks, DeLoreans, Bricklins, Studebakers, and the like, but I loved the old Fords for some reason. They were amongst the cheapest and most produced cars back in the day so you would hear quite often that FORD meant "Fix Or Repair Daily."

My dad used to have a little saying that stuck with me

through the years. He said: "A little spark, a little coil, a little spring, a little oil, a piece of tin and a two-inch board, put them together and you've got a Ford." I have this memorable rhyme printed and framed in my garage. Thanks dad.

41. STORM CLOUDS

Kimberly and David were living in Hebron, Connecticut when they got married. Our granddaughter, Tuesday, was about six years old at the time. I helped David rebuild a deck at this house, but they soon moved to a new house in Lebanon which they had built.

It was a big house on a cul-de-sac and it had more land. Kimberly always wanted to keep horses on her property and this was an attempt to have a few acres of land to do just that. It was part of their agreement when they got married.

The first child to be born to Kim and Dave was Jared. He was a healthy boy initially but developed some digestive issues in his first year of life. These medical issues were eventually overcome and he would continue to develop into the great kid that he is today.

The Lebanon house was nice but it had some construction issues that had to be corrected. One glaring issue was the brick fireplace which was visibly lopsided. What kind of mason would build something that was not perfectly straight? The builder was contacted and agreed that the fireplace had to be reconstructed. That same mason and his son were called back to correct the problem.

They tore down the brick surrounding the fireplace opening and rebuilt it. When they were done, I had a chance to check out their work and, in my estimation, the brick was still askew. These guys should find another occupation because they were certainly not cut out to be masons. I went on to help David install a wood laminate floor in their dining room at some point in the coming weeks and months.

As time went on, friction developed between them and some neighbors. Things were said and done which basically 'black balled' them in the community. One such problem between them and a police officer neighbor had to do with shrubs on the property line. Apparently, David thought they were on his property so he went out one night and moved them. Really? You don't build good relations with a neighbor by doing something underhanded and stupid like that.

Another incident involved David placing his bee hives near the property line of his neighbor. Really? The neighbor had little kids running around and, of course, was concerned for their safety.

The relationship just got worse when David burned trash in the back yard with prevailing winds blowing towards the cop's house. They called the fire department and the hostility escalated to a point where living there was becoming stressful. We were starting to see a trend with David and this marriage and it was not a good indicator of a healthy relationship.

It wasn't long after this that Kim and Dave sold the Lebanon house and bought a house in Tolland on Metcalf Road with about six acres of land. It was an old farmhouse built in the 1700's with a separate barn where Kim could stable horses. Did they finally find a place where they could all be happy?

This house would not have been my first choice, but the kids did not ask for our input. The old house had a lot of issues including electrical and heating which would have to be mitigated in the near future. It was not very well insulated and it cost a lot of money to heat it in the winter time. They were always cold, kept the house at fifty-five degrees and we just kept our coats on when visiting in the colder weather.

But Kim and Dave persisted and went on to have two more children while living at this location. Our granddaughter Lacey was the next to arrive followed by (surprise!) Piper. It seemed as though they were happy, but the storm clouds were just forming on this marriage.

They decided to build an addition on to the old farmhouse. It would be a two-story addition with a playroom and dining area downstairs and an additional bedroom upstairs which was to be for Tuesday, our oldest granddaughter. As always, I helped out where I could and got involved with this project from the beginning. I helped with framing, siding, roofing, electrical, windows and doors and, sheetrock. I worked with

David to shingle the roof of the addition as well as the entire roof of the old house. We actually worked together quite well and so we had a glimmer of hope for this marriage after all. It turned out to be a huge project and it took the good part of a year to complete. I spent an entire week just painting and installing trim work. I would do anything for my daughter, her family, and her happiness. Kim by this time had a couple of horses which really made her happy. Looking back on it, she should have become a veterinarian and married someone that had the same ambitions as her. But she made decisions in life that took her in this direction and we would all have to deal with the outcome.

We had Kim, Dave and the grandkids come to Florida several times to visit us with all expenses paid. Our first house in The Villages was nice but we eventually bought a bigger house that included a salt water pool and hot tub. The grandkids loved it here and spent upwards of thirty hours in the pool in a week's time. The noise level also increased appreciably around the lanai during their visits. The neighbors certainly knew when they were here.

When our kids came to Florida, we always rented a golf cart for them. It was a great way to get around the community and the grandkids all learned to drive a golf cart while they were here. Just let them drive the golf cart and swim in the pool and they were happy campers.

On one occasion while they were driving around our neighborhood with the kids in the back of the golf cart, David took off without checking to see if the kids were secure.

Lacey got ejected out on to the roadway and suffered some cuts and scrapes. We felt so bad for her. This is a man who was supposed to be a safety engineer. Really? We were going to have to keep a closer eye on this guy.

Storm clouds were thickening on Kim's relationship with David as he resisted her attempt to have the happy farm life that she envisioned. He was a very controlling type of person. In order to make ends meet and to earn some extra money, Kimberly trained to become a bus driver in town. Her schedule with four children could revolve around their school hours, summer vacations, and snow days. Perfect, or so it seemed.

Between this job, postpartum depression and pressure from her husband about keeping horses on the property, Kimberly finally crashed with a nervous breakdown. We stepped in at this point with a financial infusion to help them out through the coming year. It was not enough and it was not meant to be. Kimberly filed for divorce after ten years of marriage. It is very sad for me to write about this, but as parents we tried to help our children and grandchildren in any way we could. We always wanted the best for our kids through good times and bad. In the coming years, a contentious child custody battle would ensue and it continues to this day. The Metcalf house was sold and any profits went to lawyer's fees.

Kim rented a house for a couple of years in Tolland and we eventually helped her with a down payment on a house of her very own. It was good for Kim and her kids to be grounded in one place so, in that respect, the money was well spent. It's too bad that so much money was wasted on defending oneself in court instead of going to the grandkids to help out with education and other needs.

Kimberly eventually ended up in the Tolland school system teaching challenged kids as a paraprofessional. She helped many children in Tolland High School to graduate and parents of those children were eternally grateful to her. She even attended graduations for 'her kids' for which I am sure they were appreciative. She has a good heart. As of this writing, Kimberly is working towards her master's degree in Education. Her specialties are math, chemistry, and physics. She should be able to command a good salary upon completion. You go, girl!

I know she will find happiness in the future in her new relationships and profession. We are extremely proud of her. We hope that someday she can fulfill her dream of coming to Florida and having her own horse farm. She certainly deserves it after all she has been through. Happier times are coming. As far as Kim's ex-husband goes, I guess you just can't polish a turd.

42. BOATING

During my lifetime, I have had a number of boats. I started at a young age. When I was about ten years old, I wanted a boat to go fishing. I mentioned it to my dad on more than one occasion. Being an impatient little kid, I gathered up some materials and started to build a small boat in the side yard of our house. When my dad came home from work and saw what I was up to, he started laughing. He may have been laughing because my construction skills weren't too good at the time, but I must have gotten the idea across to him that I was serious about having a boat.

It wasn't too long after the boat building attempt that my dad purchased an aluminum twelve foot skiff, some oars, and a five-horsepower Clinton outboard motor. He must have gotten permission from my mom because we didn't have a lot of extra money to throw around. Times were tough. To transport the boat, dad put a bumper hitch on the car.

Richard Stoebel

Connected to that was a four-foot long pole with a clamp on the top of it which affixed to the transom of the boat. The bow was then picked up and swung onto the roof of the car, placed on a roof rack and strapped down. Other than lifting the boat to clamp to the transom, this was pretty much a one-man operation.

Dad and I did some fishing at local ponds and lakes. We caught trout, pickerel, bass, and perch. At nighttime we sometimes caught catfish which New Englanders also called horned pout. It was fun having a boat and spending time with my dad. We were 'bonding.'

When I got a little older, maybe twelve, dad let me take the boat out by myself. I found that if I cranked the 5-hpmotor up to full power and scooched forward to the center seat that I could get the old aluminum boat up on plane and travel along at a whopping twenty-five miles per hour. It wasn't really fast, but it felt that way at the time. I'm not sure when we got rid of that boat, but it was eventually sold when I got a little older. I was becoming more interested in farm work, tractors, trucks, cars, and girls, not necessarily in that order.

The next boat in my lifetime would come after I had gotten married and we had our first child, Kimberly. For some reason, the boating bug bit me again and I ended up purchasing a boat, motor, trailer combination for $750 from a guy in Wethersfield. This was a sixteen foot aluminum runabout with a 35-hp Mercury motor and we took it to Coventry Lake on nice summer days for cruising, fishing, and eating at the dockside restaurant.

Me with our runabout at Coventry Lake, Coventry, Connecticut.

I remember being out on the lake one time when we were passed by a bunch of young girls in a speedboat. In front of them was a couple of ducks with their babies swimming along and frantically trying to get out of the way of the oncoming speedboat. Instead of veering away from the birds, the girls turned in their direction in an attempt to run them over. How cruel and how stupid they were to do something like that. The incident bothered me so much that I followed them back to their dock, confronted their parents and told them what had happened. I don't know if the girls suffered any consequences, but I just couldn't let this outrageous act of harm to wildlife go without saying something.

This runabout was eventually sold for about the same price I bought it for. It was time to move on.

It was quite a few years before my next boat. I must have gotten the itch again to have one and our kids were at an age where I could take them water skiing. My boats kept

getting bigger and this time I purchased a Bayliner eighteen
-foot cuddy cabin model with an 85-hp Mercury motor. This
was an entry level boat that we used not only at Coventry
Lake, but on the Connecticut River and Long Island sound.
Brett and I had taken the safe boating course together to
get our licenses which I felt necessary if we were going
to navigate busier waters surrounded by bigger boats and
ships. It may have even been Connecticut law at that time.

During a Columbus Day vacation in October, Brett and
I launched at the Hartford ramp and drove the boat forty-
three miles down to Long Island sound. It was a nice trip,
but I remember the wind and boating traffic at the inlet
was making the water so rough, we took a wave over the
bow and into the back of the boat. Not wanting to take any
chances of getting swamped, we turned around and headed
back up stream. Brett drove the boat all the way back to
Hartford. Good job!

We were cruising Coventry Lake one day. As we passed by
the town beach and headed between the shore and an island, I
spotted something in the water ahead of us. I couldn't see it at
first because of sun glare, but I eventually spotted a swimmer's
head. An adult was swimming from shore out to the island
and stood the chance of getting hit by doing so. How stupid
to swim across open water with speedboats traveling along at
high speed on a busy weekend day. You've got to wonder why
some people do crazy things like that.

I had met a guy at work that enjoyed salt water fishing.
John talked me into taking our Bayliner down to Waterford

for a day of fishing. Brett came with us. We launched and headed past the Millstone Nuclear power plant. The warm discharge water from the facility drew in all kinds of bait fish with larger fish feeding on them.

After awhile, we headed out into deeper water to try our luck near a reef. As we were anchored there, the dreaded fog rolled in. I only had a magnetic compass on board. A depth finder and electronic navigation system sure would have come in handy at this point, but we were just bare bones.

It became evident after a couple of hours that the fog was not going to lift anytime soon. These were treacherous waters with rocky shoals and outcroppings all around us. Were we going to have to spend the night here? Just about then, a larger fishing boat came out of the fog and stopped to chat with us. They understood our dilemma and tried to help us find our way back to the boat ramp.

They gave us a magnetic compass heading that should point us in the right direction to get us back to safety. We took their advice, pulled up our anchor and headed in the prescribed direction. Luckily, we did make it back to the ramp without ramming any rocks and I learned a valuable lesson that day about boating in the ocean. Fog can be scary.

The next obstacle was to pull the boat out of the water with our Ford Thunderbird. A rear wheel drive car is not the best type of vehicle to launch and retrieve a boat on a slippery ramp. As I tried to pull the boat up the ramp, we ended up sliding backwards towards the water. Thankfully, shoveling beach sand under the wheels to get traction helped and we were finally successful in pulling the boat and trailer up the ramp. The whole car could have ended up in the water. I was relieved to get out of there and headed back home.

I sold the Bayliner and it would be a number of years before my next boat. I got the itch again and found a SeaRay twenty-four foot cabin cruiser that was for sale in Willimantic. After inspecting it, a deal was struck and I had a boat transport company move it to Spicer's Marina in Noank.

Our friends Larry and Pina Krizan had their boat in a slip there and we were lucky enough to get a slip on the same dock. I enjoyed the atmosphere of being at the shore and I enjoyed the camaraderie of the many boat owners. We took some nice cruises out to Fisher's Island and up the Mystic River to the Seaport. Navigating these waterways was a learning experience because of the rock outcroppings and hazards. Local knowledge was imperative otherwise you could damage, or, God forbid, sink your boat and jeopardize the safety of your passengers.

I owned this boat for a couple of years but found that it was difficult to handle without a crew. To drop anchor, I had to go into the cabin, open the front hatch, climb out onto the bow and deploy it. It was also awkward to tie up at the dock. I eventually traded the SeaRay for a twenty-four foot SeaPro walk around cuddy cabin that I found at a local boat store in South Windsor. It was newer and it was set up more for fishing than the previous boat.

I could handle this one by myself because of the walk around feature and access to the bow to drop anchor. I made an observation about boating that I think is prophetic in many ways and that is "no matter how big your boat is, it gets smaller and smaller the further out onto the ocean you go."

Our 24-foot SeaRay at the marina in Noank, Connecticut.

On many occasions I got out of work in Middletown at midnight and drove down to the marina to sleep over on the SeaPro which I had named "Water Hazard" (golfing term). The two person cabin was very comfortable to sleep in. One night I was just dozing off and heard a knocking noise on the hull. What the hell is that? When I got up to investigate, I realized that a swan was pecking on the boat looking for a handout. I guess people fed them and they would do that to get your attention. Pain in the ass birds.

The SeaPro turned out to be a great family boat as we spent many hours fishing, clamming, cruising, and just hanging out at the marina. One day, I had gone out into Long Island sound by myself to do some fishing. On my way back to the dock I was having difficulty maneuvering the boat and I thought it just might be the wind. After struggling to back into our slip and eventually tying up to the dock, I raised the inboard/outboard outdrive to inspect it. No wonder I was having a tough time controlling the boat because there was a line wrapped around the outdrive.

As I unwrapped the line and pulled on it, I discovered a lobster pot was still attached to it. With two big lobsters in it. Lobster pot buoys were a real hazard in the summer. They were numerous because summer residents could obtain a seasonal license to fish for lobsters. Once the summer was over, just the commercial lobster pots remained and it was much easier to navigate these waters. I returned the pot to a fisheries substation as a courtesy but, of course, I kept the lobsters which would be the main course at dinner that evening.

You know that saying "a boat is a hole in the water that you pour money into?" It's true. Boating is very expensive and extremely so when there is a fuel crisis and the cost soars to over $4 a gallon. We have gone through times like that and it makes boating not quite as much fun as in good times. They say that the two best days for owning a boat are when you buy it and when you sell it. It finally came time to part with "Water Hazard" and I listed it with the sales department at Spicer's Marina.

It wasn't long before the Marina found a potential buyer. After taking them out for a sea trial, the boat was sold and I was now boatless again. As I sat in the parking lot overlooking the marina and having lunch, I observed hundreds of boats worth millions of dollars. There were a couple of people here and there working on their boats, but the majority of them were just sitting idle waiting for their owners to visit on the weekend. This might be the last boat that I would ever own. Maybe.

43. SNOWFLAKES

I had been retired for a year or two but Brenda was still working (kind of the best of both worlds, don't you think?). We started to get more serious about our retirement plans. We were both on the same frequency in that we wanted to retire in Florida. Around the Christmas holidays of 2010, Brenda took her remaining vacation days and we headed south to look for a retirement location.

We had spent time on the east coast in the West Palm Beach area while I was still working, so now we wanted to check out the west coast of Florida. We traveled down Interstate 95 and turned right on Route 4 through Orlando and over to Tampa. Traveling south on Interstate 75, we finally reached Naples and got a hotel room for a couple of nights

Coming from New England in December, Naples felt really hot and humid to us. Why? Because it was. Sitting out near the hotel pool in the evening with a glass of wine was delightful, if you call sweating delightful. This would take some getting used to. We can see why Floridians say they would die if they went north in the winter. Blood surely thins out in this climate and it would be very difficult to acclimate to cold weather again.

We scouted around the Naples area for retirement homes but quickly realized the only things to do there were beach, golf, and boating. It was also very crowded near the ocean. Hell, with all of the high-rise buildings next to the gulf waters, you couldn't even see the beach and had limited access if you did not live right there in a condominium.

It was time to scout out the rest of the Gulf Coast. Heading north, we checked out Fort Meyers, St. Pete and Tampa, and quickly came to the same conclusion. At two o'clock in the afternoon traffic was gridlocked everywhere we went. And, again, we could not even see the beach with all the high-rise buildings blocking the view.

Clearwater Beach we found out on a later visit was very nice but the only way to enjoy it was a day trip or a stay in one of the high-priced hotels. We kept heading north to Spring Hill where our very dear friends, Larry and Pina Krizan, lived. They had inherited a house in Timber Pines from Larry's dad and decided to make that their winter escape place. It became full time in the future. This was an older retirement community and while very nice, did not have the activities we were looking for.

Next stop... The Villages (TV). We had spent a week there on the Lifestyles Program back in 2003, but we were not ready to retire at that point and the timing was just not right. This time around we had a reservation to rent in TV for a week. Our Gulf Coast excursion was coming to an early end so additional accommodations were quickly made and off we headed in that direction.

The Villages is located an hour north of Orlando and a half hour south of Ocala in central Florida. We were put up in a nice three-bedroom, two-bath villa right next to Sumter Landing town square. This town center was not yet built the last time we visited the area in 2003.

Our first house in The Villages, Florida. A Jasmine model, 1876 Ashwood Run.

Sumter Landing was modeled after a New England town and situated at the edge of a lake. There were numerous shops, restaurants, a movie theater, and entertainment nightly at the gazebo in the center of it all. Weather was a little chilly as I recall, but it was a heck of a lot warmer than Connecticut at this time of year.

During our two weeks in TV we met with a Village real

estate agent, Lori Simon, on multiple occasions. She showed us new home models and lots where we could have our dream house built. I think we had always intended to end up here because, before we left to go back to Connecticut, we put our money down on a lot and selected a house plan (The Jasmine). It was a three-bedroom, two-bath house with a two-car garage which would be more than adequate for our winter getaway.

We were told the house would be completed in three months, but we really didn't believe that it could be done that quickly. We were wrong because in March of 2010, we found ourselves flying back down to Florida for the closing. We ordered a few necessities like bedroom and living room furniture which was delivered just prior to the closing. After the deal was done, we stayed in our new house for the first time that night.

Our Florida home became a reality and our retirement plans were kicking into gear. We planned to spend the three winter months of January, February and March in Florida and the remaining time at our house in Connecticut.

The first morning after staying in our new house, we met the folks across the street from us. Mike and Diane were very welcoming neighbors and she, being the consummate southern belle from Virginia, came across the street to give us a big hug and exclaimed in her southern drawl: "I'm so glad you are not old people with walkers and canes." They were our first introduction to the neighborhood and we couldn't have been happier.

Since we didn't have anything in the new house to prepare breakfast, I drove down to Starbucks at Lake Sumter Landing to get some coffee and pastry for Brenda and me. I like my coffee light, so as I was pouring black coffee out my cup to make room for lots of cream, a lady at a high top table nearby exclaimed: "You must like coffee with your cream."

Our second house in The Villages, Florida, 2118 Lake Ridge Drive. We needed a larger place to store two hot rods and for living here full time.

She caught me a little off guard, but I was able to come back with the quick response: "Yes, but you'll notice that I'm not putting any sugar in it because I'm sweet enough already." And her reply was: "I'll bet you are." I'm not sure, but I think she may have been trying to pick me up. Maybe not. In any regard, this was the start of our retirement adventures in Florida.

We were Florida snowflakes for a very short time. We quickly became snowbirds, established residency in Florida and escaped the state income tax of Connecticut. That move saved us over $7,000.00 a year. In the ensuing years we stayed longer and longer until it finally made no sense to keep our Connecticut house which was becoming a burden.

We had progressed from being Snowflakes to Snowbirds and now became Frogs… permanent Florida residents who would croak here, It was inevitable that this progression would happen and I guess that many retirees experience the same thing. Even though our kids and grandkids were still in Connecticut, this is where we really wanted to spend our retirement years.

As snowbirds, our plan was to travel back and forth from Florida to Connecticut as the seasons changed. Maintaining two houses was not too bad and our children could come to visit us in Florida any time during the cold months that they wanted to. Eventually, as we spent more time in Florida, we decided to sell our Connecticut house and purchase a bigger one in Florida. I had two antique hot rod cars and, if they were coming to Florida, we would need a house with more garage space.

After just returning to Connecticut, I spotted a premier house on the TV website. It was not too far from our Jasmine and in the same Village of Pennecamp. We made a low-ball offer to the owners of this St. Charles model but they didn't even counter offer. We upped the offer in a stronger bid and this time the owners countered. As negotiations continued, the owners listed a kitchen faucet arrangement that would not be included in the deal which we thought was kind of strange and a little bit trite.

We communicated to the real estate agent who had listed the house that they could "keep the house and shove the kitchen faucet where the sun don't shine."

We cut off negotiations on that house and started to look elsewhere for another one. After some time had passed, perhaps a couple of weeks, I started to look at the St. Charles listing again (after a few glasses of wine I might add). We really liked this house with its expansive garage, large lanai with a salt water pool, location, and close proximity to our Jasmine. One final strong offer was proposed and accepted with the caveat that we would have one week to fly down to Florida to personally inspect the property. Upon arrival, we loved the house and made the decision to go through with the deal.

Things were moving fast now. In one week we listed our Jasmine for sale, sold it and closed on both houses. This was a hot market. The Village Movers transferred our meager belongings to the new house and said: "See you in six months."

The market was not as hot in Connecticut, but we decided to try to sell our Bella Vista Lane house on our own. We spent several months preparing it for sale and within another two months we found a buyer. We saved a lot of commission dollars by selling both of our most recent Connecticut houses by ourselves. We were now down to owning just one house. This gave us the opportunity to rent vacation property at the Rhode Island and Connecticut shore during the summer to spend quality time with our kids and grandkids in a grand way.

We spent our first summer weeks in Rhode Island at Misquamicut Beach and Green Hill Beach. Later summers were spent at Milford, Fairfield and Mystic, Connecticut beaches.

We have collected many memories of these precious days with our children and grandchildren. These were all quality visits and they in turn came to Florida for Thanksgiving and Christmas holidays. Sometimes they came multiple times during the winter when they had had enough of cold, ice, and snow. This arrangement was working wonderfully and we were settling in to our retirement lifestyle.

Life was good!

44. DANCING & TRAVEL

During our travels as Snowflakes, Snowbirds and Frogs, we visited some interesting places and attractions. We were not international travelers by any stretch of the imagination and just enjoyed experiencing things within the country. On our trips back and forth from Florida to Connecticut, we visited places like Savannah, Georgia including a horse and carriage ride through the historic district. Another stop further up the coast was in Charleston, South Carolina and a visit to one of the many plantations in the area.

One of my favorite stops was on the outer banks of North Carolina at Kill Devil Hills. This national historic site is where the Wright Brothers flew the first powered airplane flights in 1903. The museum there has a replica of the Wright Flyer based on the original which is located at the Smithsonian Institute in Washington, DC.

On other trips up and down the east coast, we spent a

couple of days at the Biltmore Mansion in Asheville, North Carolina. It was constructed for George Vanderbilt in 1895 as a summer home. The vineyards and hills around this estate are breathtaking.

Brenda had always wanted to visit Amish country around Lancaster, Pennsylvania, so we made a stop on one of our trips to Connecticut for a tour. We were loaded into a horse drawn carriage. It was a chilly morning so we were offered a heavy, handmade wool blanket to put over our laps. That really kept us warm as we trotted around the beautiful countryside.

One of our stops was at a local Amish working farm. We did not get to meet the women and girls as they were off on an errand, but we did get to meet the man of the house and his boys. The older boy, perhaps sixteen years of age, was mowing the lawn with a hand pushed mower. I used to do that when I was a kid so I know how much work it is.

The younger son, Daniel, maybe ten years old was busy grooming one of their horses and applying dressing to its hooves. After some small talk with the father, the boys gave us a tour of the store in the basement of their house where they had handmade items for sale. I remember Daniel staring at Brenda's diamond rings because he had never seen anything like that in the simple lifestyle that they lived. I'm quite sure his mother didn't have any rings like that.

We bought some jams and jellies to give to our children. As we got back into the carriage and started to pull away, there was Daniel in the barn waving a courteous goodbye to us. How cute was that? It is an image in my mind that I still cherish to this day. I admire the simple lifestyle that the Amish folks have because it is not polluted with television and outside influences that our families are all subjected to today. Maybe they've got it right after all. God bless them.

We have taken local trips around Florida. There are so many interesting things to see right in this state. We spent a couple of days in St. Augustine. It is the nation's oldest city and was founded many years before Jamestown and the pilgrims landing at Plymouth Rock.

A must visit place is Ponce de Leon's Fountain of Youth. During a tour of the archaeological site, we sampled the much acclaimed water. My conclusion is that it might add some years to your life, but it tastes like shit. Nearby is the Spanish Fort, Castillo de San Marcos, which is over 315 years old. This is a very interesting national monument to tour and comes with the occasional demonstration of firing a cannon. We have yet to see the beach at St. Augustine, so a return trip is surely on the agenda.

It is hard to imagine how big a state Florida is until you drive down to Key West. From north central Florida it took us almost seven hours, with a few stops, to get there. We stayed overnight in Marathon Key and drove the remaining half hour out to Key West for the day. A necessary visit was paid to the Ernest Hemmingway house as well as the southernmost point in the United States which is only ninety miles from Cuba. Stray chickens and roosters were everywhere in town which was strange and interesting. It must be a Cuban influence thing?

The turquoise waters and white, white sands are just beautiful to behold and the old architecture of buildings and homes are very, well, Key West. It was evident to me that there is a large contingent of LBGTQ here and I suppose that goes with the artistic nature of the community. I guess I am okay with that. Live and let live.

Back in Marathon, I had my first and only taste of fried key lime pie. It was superb. Try it sometime if you have a chance. You won't be disappointed.

We always wanted to take a trip to New Orleans. Our kids had been there, but we had never taken the opportunity to visit. We looked at tours that were available through local agencies. One such trip was the music city tour which included New Orleans, Memphis and Nashville.

We had already been to Nashville when our kids were bike racing, so we didn't feel the need to go there again. We decided to take a road trip on our own for a week and see the sights. We wanted to see the panhandle region of Florida, so this was our chance to explore.

The first day of our trip brought us to Fort Walton Beach. This Gulf Coast area is nicknamed the "Emerald Strand" because of its beautiful water and endless beaches. We parked the car and walked the beach which was very crowded. Local people told us that this coastal area used to be pristine but with the building of high-rise condominiums, the crowds and traffic increased dramatically. It was an economic boom for the area, but it changed the landscape forever in the name of progress.

The next day we were off to New Orleans, Louisiana. We stayed at the Hotel Provincial in the French Quarter. We were pleasantly surprised at our accommodations smack dab in the middle of all the activity. We really enjoyed the Hurricane cocktails at the bar in the evening.

From this hotel, we took a carriage ride around the historic district. Our driver was a blue-eyed black man who was very knowledgeable about the area. He had been born and raised here. The blue eyes came from intermixing of French and black backgrounds. The carriages were not drawn by horses, but mules that were more tolerant of the heat and humidity.

We paid a visit to the WWII Museum nearby which was very interesting to me. The display of airplanes in one dedicated building was amazing. One evening, we booked a sunset dinner cruise on the steamboat *Natchez*. A Dixieland band entertained us after dinner as we cruised along the Mississippi River on a spectacular evening. Check another item off our to-do list.

On our last night in New Orleans, we strolled through the French Quarter. As we came upon the Balcony Music Club, we heard the band inside playing a tune that was perfect for swing dancing. I asked Brenda if she would like to dance. Of course she said: "Yes, I'd love to," so we sauntered into the establishment.

There were people drinking and dining in the raised areas around the dance floor, but no one was dancing. Brenda put her pocketbook down on the edge of the stage and we began to dance in our favorite east coast swing style. All of a sudden, we noticed that people had their phones out and were taking video of us. Someone said: "You guys are good and you're going to be on YouTube. How much fun would that be? After the song ended, we applauded the band, Brenda picked up her pocketbook and we continued our evening stroll. That dance was so memorable for us and is a highlight of this trip that we will remember forever.

The next day it was off to Memphis where we stayed at the Graceland Hotel. They had a theater within the complex where we watched Elvis movies both evenings that we were there. We booked a VIP tour of Graceland and the museum the next day which was led by a very knowledgeable young lady who had been born and brought up in the area. It was a good thing we had an expert tour guide because she explained things to us that we would have just walked by or ignored.

Elvis Presley was not a favorite of mine when I was growing up, but I have come to realize what a talented person he was. There is a wall in the museum that is filled with hundreds of his awards and it is truly impressive. After taking this tour, I am now an Elvis fan.

I could write a whole chapter about dancing. I have always loved music and Brenda has always loved dancing. We started dancing together seriously by taking country partner lessons from a couple named Bill and Miriam Cover at the Pratt and Whitney facility on Clement Road in East Hartford, Connecticut. It is there that we met good friends Bob and Charlotte White. Together and with our group, we put on shows at country fairs and nursing homes. We either took lessons or went out to dance four times a week, and we were still working full time.

We met many nice people doing this activity. Over the years, we learned two step, waltz, partner, and line dances. We had a log book with the steps to more than sixty dances in it. I'm not sure how we remembered them all. When we came to The Villages in retirement, we started to take east coast swing dance lessons every week from a nice couple: Kermit and Carol.

East coast swing quickly became our favorite dance and we went on to learn many variations of the genre. That is why, when we were in New Orleans, we were so comfortable dancing in front of a bunch of strangers on a deserted dance floor. It was a feeling of confidence. We continue to take all kinds of dance lessons to this day. I suppose you never stop learning which is a good thing to keep the mind and body active.

Our first cruise on a ship was years ago with our friends, Charlotte and Bob. We were into country dancing at the time and a "country cruise" was being held on a Norwegian Cruise Lines (NCL) ship named, appropriately, *Norway*. This was an eastern Caribbean cruise to the US Virgin Islands, St. Martin and St. Johns.

My first impression when we anchored off one of the islands was the beautiful, turquoise water and the volcanically formed topography of the land. Once on shore though, it was evident that there were very rich people and very poor people who inhabited the islands. There was no middle class.

The rich folks had beautiful homes up on the hillside

overlooking the ocean and the poor ones lived in shacks. To me, the beauty of the trip was seen mostly from the ship. The *Norway* was an older ship that had been remodeled many times and it was a 1,000 foot long beauty. It wasn't too many years later that the ship was being outclassed by more modern ones and the *Norway* was taken to India where it was decommissioned and reduced to scrap metal.

Our second cruise came years later when we resided in Florida. We took a trip with Royal Caribbean on their huge *Oasis of the Seas* to the western Caribbean. Ports of call included Nassau (an emergency to offload a person with a medical emergency), Jamaica, Haiti, and Cozumel. In my old age I am not a very adventurous person, so we passed up most shore excursions except for the one in Labadie, Haiti. The port in Labadie was created and controlled by the cruise line, so it was relatively safe to explore the immediate area.

I had always wanted to swim and snorkel in the Caribbean so we booked an excursion that took us by boat to a remote beach where we could relax, swim, snorkel, and have a couple of included drinks. It was a beautiful location as we had expected and I finally got to swim in the Caribbean. The snorkeling equipment was not very good quality, so that adventure would have to wait.

Part of the excursion included a walking tour of a Haitian village in which we participated. As we climbed a crude staircase up the hillside next to the shore, there was an outhouse. I knew it was a crapper long before we got there because I could smell it. The effluent discharging from it was draining directly into the bay we had just swum in. Now we were seeing the real Haiti. The village was no surprise either as some visibly poor local people were hand making small items for sale and selling candy to make a few dollars. Okay, time to get out of here and back to the ship.

Cozumel was a tourist trap, but we got off the ship just to say we had been there. We could see slums with blue tarps covering roofs in the distance from our vantage point high on the ship. I wasn't impressed with the Caribbean as a whole and realized, once again, we have it made right here in the good old USA. We may sign up for another cruise someday. I would like to see the Panama Canal and maybe Alaska. They are both on the bucket list.

My observation from the limited cruising we have done is that there are a lot of really large, overweight people on these ships. I'm thinking that it must be the limitless buffets, food, and deserts that are available around the clock that attracts them. This reminds me of a saying from my dear old dad which goes "there are a lot more horses' asses than there are horses." He was right and I'm starting to realize that he was a great, undiscovered philosopher. Thanks, dad, for all of these great sayings. I will be passing them on to my kids and grandkids. I'll even pass them on to my great grandkids if we become so blessed.

45. THE VILLAGES

So here we are now living in our retirement community in Florida. I reflect back on my humble beginnings growing up in central Massachusetts and the encouragement I received from my folks so that I could have a good life and probably a better one than they had. I think of my dad's passing and how devastating that was to me. I should have been there for him.

I still remember the violent thunderstorm that passed through my home town of Clinton, Massachusetts at the exact hour of his death. Was it a sign from above? After the funeral, my mother was holding on to my arm as we approached his gravesite at Woodlawn cemetery. Mom gasped as she realized that the cemetery crew had opened up the wrong burial location. Her words were: "Those damn Irishmen can't get anything right." I chuckle when I think of that moment. Dad was eighty-four years old when he passed,

We went back later that day for a second attempt to bury him and this time the Irishmen got it right.

Mom had many more good years after my dad's passing and made it to the ripe old age of ninety-three. Again, I regret to this day that I was not with her when she passed. I suppose it all worked out the way it did because of divine intervention. I guess I will never know for sure. She suffered from a burst intestine and succumbed one week after an emergency operation.

Mother had been transported from our small hometown hospital in Clinton, by helicopter, to the University of Massachusetts Hospital in Worcester. Even as sick as she was, she teased me that she had gotten a ride in a helicopter before me. She knew that was on my bucket list. Thanks for poking me, Mom. Mother is buried in Woodlawn cemetery next to my dad. And, yes, she is in the correct burial spot. God rest her soul.

Brenda lost her dad, Joe Gosselin, at the age of seventy-six. He suffered from lung cancer. Looking back on it, Joe was really a hero. He had served as a teenager in the Army in Panama. He was a golden gloves boxer. He had no fear.

He served his country again during WWII with the Navy in the Pacific. He was assigned to an LST ship which landed troops and equipment at various Pacific island battles. He took part in defending against Kamakaze attacks at sea and told me of his experience shooting down a Japanese Zero that almost hit his ship. He witnessed an ammunition ship in his convoy getting blown up and sinking with all men on board.

The tremendous explosion damaged his hearing for life.

One of the more humorous stories from his Navy service was about the ship mascot, Bonzo. The captain's pet monkey was allowed to roam the ship and he occasionally crapped in Joe's bunk bed. Joe had enough of that and one evening while on guard duty, Bonzo went overboard. He wisely never told anyone on ship what he had done.

We celebrate Joe's service with a picture of him in his Navy uniform next to a wall mounted display case with a tri-fold flag and his original honorable discharge papers. Being the daredevil that he was, when he was seventy-four he mounted our daughter's horse, took it around the indoor rink and urged it over a large jump. Joe flew with me on several occasions and when I handed the controls to him, he handled the airplane like he had been born to do it.

Brenda's sister, Karen, died from stomach cancer when she was in her forties. I don't think Brenda's mom ever got over the loss of that child. Karen's daughter, Nicole, lived with us under our guardianship for a number of years. We did everything for that girl that we could do to help her grow up in the absence of her biological mom. We probably did more for her than we did for our own children. I hope she realizes someday how we sacrificed and, hopefully, influenced her path through life in a good way.

Brenda's mom, Bridget passed from this life when she was ninety-three. We were at her bedside when she slipped away. I had never experienced being with someone when they died. Looking back, I should have been there for my mom and dad at their moment of passing. Sometimes I wish I could turn back the clock and do it all over again. I would have done certain things in my life differently, that is for sure.

De Havilland Beaver, Pratt & Whitney R985 engine, Mount Dora, Florida.

On the lighter side, I still have a passion for flying. On a trip to Mount Dora recently, we met the pilot of a DeHaviland Beaver who was giving rides from the dock of the old hotel. I always wanted to fly a float plane and I always wanted to fly behind a Pratt & Whitney radial engine. This plane would knock off two of my bucket list items in one shot. I made a reservation with the understanding that I would actually like to fly the plane from the copilot seat. The pilot agreed and after takeoff he said: "Your airplane."

I climbed to 1,000 feet, trimmed the elevator and flew the headings that were given to me. The heavy aircraft was actually very light on the controls but it was also very noisy behind that throbbing radial engine. Headsets and intercom helped with communication. After a half-hour flight, I turned the controls back over to the pilot and he made a perfect landing on the lake. I was able to enter the time in my logbook and I bought a tee shirt that read "I rode the Beaver." Some people will see the humor in that and some will not.

Brenda, knowing my still burning passion for airplanes, gave me a recent birthday gift of a flight in a biplane. This had been on my bucket list for some time and she took the initiative to gift me with this booking. It was a flight in a 1940 Waco UPF-7 hangered at Merritt Island, Florida near Cocoa Beach. After having been postponed a couple of times due to inclement weather, I finally got a date to fly on a good day.

We stayed overnight in Cocoa Beach and went to the airport late in the morning. My pilot in command was Lieutenant Colonel John Black who had accumulated over 3,600 hours of flight time in an Air Force F-15 Eagle. I would be in good hands flying with this guy. I had done aerobatics in my Cub and a Cessna 150 before, but this would be the first time I wore a parachute. I secretly hoped we wouldn't have to use them.

We took off with me strapped into the front cockpit and John in the back. As we flew out towards the coast, John directed me over the intercom to take over the controls.

Along the way, he had me do some gentle turns while maintaining altitude. The feeling of handling the controls quickly came back to me from my past experience of flying several hundred hours in light aircraft. After flying near Kennedy Space Center and Port Canaveral where cruise ships were docked, I turned out over the ocean and flew parallel to the shoreline.

Brenda and me with the 1940 WACO UPF-7 biplane, Merritt Island, Florida

John took over the controls, injected some oil into the exhaust to put out a smoke trail to get the attention of people on the beach below and started into a series of wingovers which were exhilarating to say the least. Next up was a barrel roll followed by a big loop and another barrel role. All of this was being video recorded by a GoPro camera attached to a strut in front of me. We were going to be on YouTube.

John then turned the controls back over to me. As we headed inland, I was instructed to do some more steep turns and a series of wingovers which I was getting pretty good at. In all, I got over a half-hour of stick time in the Waco and enjoyed every exciting minute of it. In the video, I have a shiteating grin from ear to ear on my face from takeoff to landing. This would go down in history as a great experience and I have to thank Brenda for making one of my dreams come true.

John Black also flies two-seat P51 Mustangs out of Kissimmee, Florida. Maybe a flight in a P51 is in my future, too? Next up, though, is a helicopter ride which we have booked for a later date. This is another birthday present from my lovely wife. Thanks again, Brenda.

Every day in retirement is a gift. Other than some minor health issues, we still are lucky enough to enjoy a whole host of activities like dancing, golf, pickleball, swimming, bicycling, playing with hot rod cars, flying radio-controlled airplanes, shooting, and enjoying the company of our neighbors and friends.

Speaking of neighbors, Tom and Linda across the street from us recently completed building a RV-10 airplane in their garage. I helped to install the engine and worked on some other assembly chores. There are all kinds of interesting people in our neighborhood.

Our calendar is always full of activities, which is a good thing. Giving back to the community is important to us, so we volunteer to help at the St. Vincent DePaul food pantry in Wildwood a few times a month. This is a rewarding experience and there are so many charitable people that give to this vital resource for underprivileged folks in the community. I was astonished to learn that there are over 40,000 people living in poverty in the Ocala forest just to the north of The Villages. We truly live in 'the bubble' because not far away from us there are a lot of folks struggling to just exist. What a sad situation it is that we cannot take care of our own but yet there is a national political element that wants to open borders to let more undocumented people flood into our country.

It just doesn't make sense to me but I guess that is an example of modern politics. My dad used to say: "I wouldn't trust a politician any further than I could throw a piano, and that ain't too far." More words of wisdom from Henry Stoebel.

I began writing this book with the thought that I have lived a pretty interesting life and have experienced some unique things along the way. Because I am in the twilight years of my life and almost part of becoming history myself, I decided that I'd better write down some of these things before it's too late. It still amazes me that the human mind can remember so much detail from decades ago, but can't remember what happened the previous day. I think it may have something to do with all of the many storage files in one's brain, so it takes longer to process current events.

Anyhow, I plan to publish these chapters into a book so that my kids, grandkids, and maybe great grandkids someday can have a little insight into their relative past. Probably they won't even care, maybe they will. My hope is that readers outside of our family circle may find this book interesting as well. Heck, some parts of it might be included in a movie or documentary someday. Only time will tell.

As a young person, I was never really interested in learning about history. History became more interesting to me the older I got. Now I am almost part of it. God bless the generations that follow in my footsteps and I pray that they have as good a life as I have experienced. I believe that we lived in the best of times. I was able to marry the girl of my dreams and together we made a wonderful life together.

I'm a lucky guy.

THE END

ABOUT THE AUTHOR

Richard "Dick" Stoebel lived the American Dream in mid-century America. He grew up in a modest New England home, worked during high school, married a beautiful woman, became an engineer working on jet engines, had two children, rebuilt old cars, and flew his own airplane. Like many Americans over the years, he finished building a house for his young family—six months of hands-on, never-ending evening and weekend projects.

While looking back, he also keeps his bucket list solidly in view: fly a helicopter, write a book (check off that one!), cruise the Panama Canal, live to see great grandchildren.

Now retired in Florida, Dick continues to enjoy the American Dream.

He hopes that you enjoy reading his book as much as he enjoyed writing it.

ACKNOWLEDGMENTS

Thanks to my children, Kimberly and Brett, for understanding that a parent makes mistakes and learns how to nurture a family as he goes along. Thanks also for providing some of the entertainment, stories and memories in this book.

Thanks to Pat and Chris Beltrami for being good friends and for their expertise in providing photo enhancements included in this book.

Thanks to my editor, Joyce Wedge, for straightening out my grammar and punctuation; to John Prince and Hallard Press for providing the expertise to lead me through the book publication process and for trying to make me a pro author.

Made in the USA
Columbia, SC
03 February 2022

55172707R00202